CLAUDIA QUINTANILLA

Making Memories

25 TIMELESS KNITTING PATTERNS FOR CHILDREN

Hardie Grant

BOOKS

To my grandmother Rosa: where everything started!

CONTENTS

> '**SCIENTISTS SAY THAT HUMAN BEINGS ARE MADE OF ATOMS, BUT A LITTLE BIRD TOLD ME THAT WE ARE ALSO MADE OF STORIES**'
>
> — EDUARDO GALEANO

THIS BOOK BEGAN as a labour of love and grief on the day I received news that my grandmother had passed away in my home country of El Salvador. It was in April of 2020, during the early stages of the Covid-19 pandemic, and like many others who had family members pass away during this time, I was unable to travel. I could not be with her in her final hours, I could not fly to El Salvador to attend her funeral nor mourn with my family.

MY GRANDMOTHER WAS much more of a mother to me than a grandparent, and my grief was profound. Trying to deal with this immense sadness, not only at her passing but also at being separated from my family, I found myself drawn to knitting. It has always been my primary method of relieving stress and anxiety. Keeping my hands busy usually helps to clear my head, but this time my mind was flooded with memories of my childhood home and relationships.

GROWING UP, I had only my family and whatever creative activities I could find to pass the time. My grandmother took note of my interest in creating, and she was always willing and happy to facilitate whatever I wanted to focus on next. My creativity bloomed, and I always found the most enjoyment in life when letting my ideas run wild, whether I was cooking, drawing, sewing or knitting. I was not the most talented at everything I tried — but even if I served up a half-burnt plate of mystery ingredients, my grandmother would dutifully take a spoonful and kindly encourage me to try again.

ALONG WITH MY grandmother, my mother and aunts gave me the skills I would need to make my visions a reality. They grew up in a convent, so had been formally trained in all things homely. In El Salvador, that mostly involved embroidery, sewing and crochet, as the climate was too hot for knitwear. They created beautiful works of art that I could only dream of making. They were inspirations, especially when it came to creating pieces for children and babies. I distinctly remember that when a new baby was born or a child's birthday was around the corner, the question between these women was never 'What are you going to buy?' but rather, 'What are you going to make?'

IT WAS WHEN my aunt had her first child that I embarked on my first successful — albeit destructive — project. At eleven years old, I asked my grandmother if I could use her ancient sewing machine to create a garment for my newborn cousin. Pressing my feet down on the large metal pedal of her creaky Singer, I began to sew the pink cotton into the most extravagant dress I could imagine — puffy sleeves, and a flouncy bottom to match. I presented the dress to my grandparents, aunts and uncles, and saw a mix of angry looks and suppressed laughs. While my grandmother was not happy that I had 'repurposed' the frilly pink curtains hanging in my bedroom window, nothing more was said. The dress looked both ridiculous and lovely, and I proudly paraded my creation, taking my cousin on a stroller walk in her new dress.

I CARRIED ON this tradition of creating clothes for little ones into my adulthood, as I myself became a parent. Even though I had learned to knit when I was a child, I rediscovered its magic after arriving in Canada and I have been in love with it ever since. Over the years, I have been honoured to share my creations with knitters across the world, including with the women who were so important in developing my love for crafting in the first place — women such as my grandmother, who supported me throughout my life, whatever passions I might be following.

AFTER MY GRANDMOTHER passed away, I felt alone in many ways, but knitting brought these memories vividly to mind. They comforted me, made me laugh, made me cry, and ultimately they inspired me to create the garments reproduced here. I hope everyone who finds themselves with this book in hand can find comfort in the process of creating, whether that be through recalling long-forgotten memories of loved ones, or creating new memories between you and the little ones in your life.

Claudia Q

COMMON ABBREVIATIONS

approx. Approximately

bef Before

beg Begin(ning)

BO Bind off

BOR Beginning of round

CDD Central double decrease: Slip 2 stitches together as if to knit to your right-hand needle. Knit the next stitch. Pass the slipped stitches over the knitted stitch. (2 stitches decreased)

ch Chain

CN Cable needle

CO Cast on

cont Continue(s), continuing

dc Double crochet

dec(d) Decrease(d)

DPN(s) Double pointed needle(s)

MDS Make double stitch: Slip the next stitch with yarn in front. Bring the yarn over the right needle to the back and pull on the slipped stitch until it looks like double stitch (two legs).

est Establish(ed)

foll(s) Follow(s)

inc(d) Increase(d)

k Knit

k1tbl Knit through back loop of the stitch (twisted stitch)

k2tog Knit 2 stitches together (1 stitch decreased)

kwise Knitwise

kfb Knit into the front of the stitch without dropping it from the needle, then knit into the back of the same stitch, then drop it from the needle (1 stitch increased)

LHN Left-hand needle

m Marker

m1l(p) Make 1 left: With your left-hand needle pick up the bar between the last stitch you knitted (purled) and the next stitch on the left-hand needle, bringing the needle from the front to the back, knit (purl) into the back of the stitch you just picked up (1 stitch increased).

m1r Make 1 right: With your left-hand needle pick up the bar between the last stitch you knitted and the next stitch on the left-hand needle, bringing the needle from the back to the front, knit into the front of the stitch you just picked up (1 stitch increased).

N / N1 / N2, etc. Needle / needle 1 / needle 2, etc.

p Purl

p1tbl Purl through back loop of the stitch (twisted stitch)

p2tog purl 2 stitches together (1 stitch decreased)

patt Pattern

pl Place

PM Place marker

psso Pass slipped stitch over (1 stitch decreased)

PUW Pick up wrap: Insert right needle upwards through the wrap around the bottom of the next stitch and the front leg of the next stitch. On a purl row, insert right needle from the back of your work through the wrap around the bottom of the next stitch and the front leg of the next stitch. Purl the two loops as if they were one stitch. On a knit row, insert needle from the front of your work. Knit the two loops as if they were one stitch.

pwise Purlwise

rem Remain(ing)

rep Repeat

RHN Right-hand needle

RM Remove marker

rnd(s) Round(s)

RS Right side of fabric

sc Single crochet

sl Slip

SM Slip marker

sp Space

ssk Slip, slip knit: Slip 2 stitches one at a time as if to knit, knit them together through back loops (1 stitch decreased)

sssk Slip, slip, slip, knit: Slip 3 stitches one at a time as if to knit, knit them together through back loops (2 stitches decreased)

st(s) Stitch(es)

St St Stockinette stitch

tbl through the back of loop

tog Together

w&t Wrap & turn: Slip the next stitch on your left needle to the right needle. If you are on a knit row, bring the yarn from back to front; if you are on a purl row, bring the yarn from front to back. Slip the stitch back to your left needle so that the yarn 'wraps' that stitch, then turn your work so the other side is facing you.

WS Wrong side of fabric

wyib With yarn in back

wyif With yarn in front

yo Yarn over

- Repeat from * to *

If I had been a better embroiderer when my daughter
was still a child, this cardigan would have been for her.
The arching flowers, applied by my dear friend Midori,
are a beautiful addition to an otherwise everyday, soft knit.

CLAUDITA

SIZES

0–3 mos (3–6 mos, 6–12 mos, 12–18 mos, 2 yr) (4 yr, 6 yr, 8 yr, 10 yr)
Recommended ease: 2″ / 5 cm of positive ease at chest

FINISHED MEASUREMENTS

Chest Circumference: 16 (18, 20, 22, 24) (26, 28, 30, 32)″ / 40.5 (45.5, 51, 56, 61) (66, 71, 76.25, 81.25) cm
Yoke Depth (front): 3.5 (4, 4.5, 5, 5) (5.5, 6, 6.5, 7)″ / 9 (10, 11.5, 12.75, 12.75) (14, 15.25, 16.5, 17.75) cm
Body Length to Underarm (at front): 3 (3.5, 4, 4.5, 5.5) (6, 6.5, 7, 7.5)″ / 7.5 (9, 10, 11.5, 14) (15.25, 16.5, 17.75, 19) cm
Upper Arm Circumference: 6.5 (7, 8, 8.25, 9) (9.75, 10.5, 11, 11.25)″ / 16 (17, 20, 21, 23) (25, 26, 27, 28) cm
Sleeve Length to Underarm: 5 (5.25, 6.25, 7.25, 7.75) (9.25, 10.5, 12, 13)″ / 13 (13, 16, 18, 19) (23, 26, 30, 33) cm

MATERIALS

Yarn:
Pink version shown in size 4 yr on Amanda (height 38″ / 97 cm)
2 (3, 3, 4, 4) (5, 6, 7, 8) skeins of 2 Ply Jumper Weight by Jamieson & Smith (100% shetland wool, 125 yds / 115 m – 25 g), colourway 003

Yellow version (without embroidery) shown in size 6 yr on Ilana (height 38″ / 97 cm)
1 (1, 1, 1, 2) (2, 2, 2, 3) skein(s) of The Uncommon Thread BFL Fingering (100% BFL, 437 yds / 400 m – 100 g), colourway Golden Praline

Or 225 (275, 325, 400, 500) (600, 700, 825, 925) yds / 205 (250, 300, 365, 450) (550, 640, 750, 845) m of fingering-weight yarn

Needles: US 5 / 3.75 mm 16″ / 40 cm circular needles (optional), 24″ / 60 cm and a set of DPNs. US 6 / 4 mm 16″ / 40 cm circular needles (optional), 24″ / 60 cm and a set of DPNs

Notions: Stitch markers, stitch holders or waste yarn, tapestry needle, 5 (5, 6, 6, 7) (7, 7, 7, 7) small buttons, embroidery needle, Temaricious embroidery threads: 1 skein each of colourways Avocado, Indigo, Kudzu Vine, Logwood, Mugwort, Pale Green

GAUGE

22 sts x 30 rows to 4″ / 10 cm on US 6 / 4 mm needles in St St, after blocking

NOTES

Sleeve instructions are written for DPNs. However, an alternate method of working small circumferences, such as Magic-Loop Method or short circular needles, can be used for the larger sizes. As the yoke increases, change to longer circular needles when necessary.

INSTRUCTIONS

The cardigan is worked from the top down with a circular yoke. A small section of short rows is worked at the back of the neck and above the hem for a more comfortable fit. Embroidery using embroidery threads is worked from a diagram.

BODY

NECKBAND
With US 5 / 3.75 mm 24″ / 60 circular needles, CO 55 (61, 67, 75, 79) (87, 91, 95, 101) sts using the Long-Tail CO Method, or your preferred method. You will continue to work flat.

Row 1 (RS): *K1, p1* to last st, k1.
Row 2 (WS): P1, *k1, p1* to end.
Rep rows 1 and 2, 1 (1, 1, 1, 1) (1, 2, 2, 2) more time(s). Rep row 1 once more.

Change to US 6 / 4 mm 24″ / 60 circular needles and work as foll:
Next Row (WS): K.

Sizes 0–3 mos, 3–6 mos, 6–12 mos, 12–18 mos, 2 yr, 4 yr and 8 yr only
Adjustment Row: K10 (9, 9, 5, 9) (3, –, 8, –, *m1l, k9 (7, 6, 5, 4) (6, –, 3, –)* to last 0 (3, 4, 0, 6) (0, –, 6, –) st(s), k to end. [60 (68, 76, 89, 95) (101, –, 122, –) sts]

Sizes 6 yr and 10 yr only
Adjustment Row: K– (–, –, –, –) (–, 7, –, 2), *m1l, k3, m1l, k4* to last – (–, –, –, –) (–, 7, –, 1) st(s), m1l, k to end. [– (–,–, –, –) (–, 114, –, 130) sts]

All sizes resume
WORK BACK NECK SHAPING
Short Row 1 (WS): P48 (54, 58, 66, 73) (80, 87, 97, 105), turn.
Short Row 2 (RS): MDS, k35 (39, 39, 42, 50) (58, 59, 71, 79), turn.
Short Row 3 (WS): MDS, p to 4 (4, 4, 4, 4) (5, 5, 5, 6) sts bef the DS, turn.
Short Row 4 (RS): MDS, k to 4 (4, 4, 4, 4) (5, 5, 5, 6) sts bef the DS, turn.
Rep short rows 3 and 4, 1 (1, 1, 1, 2) (2, 2, 3, 3) more time(s).
Next Row (WS): MDS, p to end of row, working the DSs as one (like a p2tog). [60 (68, 76, 89, 95) (101, 114, 122, 130) sts]

Sizes 0–3 mos, 3–6 mos and 6–12 mos only
Inc Row: K2, *m1l, k2* to end, and at same time, work the rem DSs as one (like a k2tog). [89 (101, 113, –, –) (–, –, –, –) sts]
Next Row: P.
Work 6 (6, 8, –, –) (–, –, –, –) rows in St St.
Inc Row: K2, *m1l, k3* to end. [118 (134, 150, –, –) (–, –, –, –) sts]
Next Row: P.
Work 6 (6, 8, –, –) (–, –, –, –) rows in St St.
Inc Row: K3, *m1l, k4* to last 3 sts, m1l, k3. [147 (167, 187, –, –) (–, –, –, –) sts]
Next Row: P.
Work 4 (8, 8, –, –) (–, –, –, –) rows in St St.

Sizes 12–18 mos, 2 yr and 4 yr only
Inc Row: K2, *m1l, k3* to end, and at same time, work the rem DSs as one (like a k2tog). [– (–, –, 118, 126) (134, –, –, –) sts]
Next Row: P.
Work – (–, –, 6, 6) (8, –, –, –) rows in St St.
Inc Row: K3, *m1l, k4* to last 3 sts, m1l, k3. [– (–, –, 147, 157) (167, –, –, –) sts]
Next Row: P.
Work – (–, –, 6, 6) (8, –, –, –) rows in St St.
Inc Row: K3, *m1l, k5* to last 4 sts, m1l, k4. [– (–, –, 176, 188) (200, –, –, –) sts]

Next Row: P.
Work – (–, –, 6, 6) (8, –, –, –) rows in St St.
Inc Row: K4, *m1l, k6* to last 4 sts, m1l, k4. [– (–, –, 205, 219) (233, –, –, –) sts]
Next Row: P.
Work – (–, –, 8, 8) (6, –, –, –) rows in St St.

Sizes 6 yr, 8 yr and 10 yr only
Inc Row: K3, *m1l, k4* to last 3 sts, m1l, k3, and at same time, work the rem DSs as one (like a k2tog). [– (–, –, –, –) (–, 142, 152, 162) sts]
Next Row: P.
Work – (–, –, –, –) (–, 6, 6, 8) rows in St St.
Inc Row: K3, *m1l, k5* to last 4 sts, m1l, k4. [– (–, –, –, –) (–, 170, 182, 194) sts]
Next Row: P.
Work – (–, –, –, –) (–, 6, 6, 8) rows in St St.
Inc Row: K4, *m1l, k6* to last 4 sts, m1l, k4. [– (–, –, –, –) (–, 198, 212, 226) sts]
Next Row: P.
Work – (–, –, –, –) (–, 6, 6, 8) rows in St St.
Inc Row: K4, *m1l, k7* to last 5 sts, m1l, k5. [– (–, –, –, –) (–, 226, 242, 258) sts]
Next Row: P.
Work – (–, –, –, –) (–, 6, 6, 8) rows in St St.
Inc Row: K5, *m1l, k8* to last 5 sts, m1l, k5. [– (–, –, –, –) (–, 254, 272, 290) sts]
Next Row: P.
Work – (–, –, –, –) (–, 8, 10, 6) rows in St St.

All sizes resume
Adjustment Row: K, dec 3 (9, 9, 13, 11) (7, 12, 16, 18) sts evenly spaced around. [144 (158, 178, 192, 208) (226, 242, 256, 272) sts]
P 1 row.

DIVIDE FOR BODY
Next Row (RS): K19 (22, 24, 27, 29) (32, 34, 37, 40), pl next 33 (35, 40, 42, 45) (49, 52, 54, 56) sts from left sleeve on to waste yarn, using Backwards Loop Method, CO 3 (3, 4, 4, 5) (5, 6, 6, 6) sts for left underarm, k across next 40 (44, 50, 54, 60) (64, 70, 74, 80) sts for back, pl next 33 (35, 40, 42, 45) (49, 52, 54, 56) sts from right sleeve on to waste yarn, using Backwards Loop Method, CO 3 (3, 4, 4, 5) (5, 6, 6, 6) sts for right underarm, k to end. [84 (94, 106, 116, 128) (138, 150, 160, 172) sts]
Next Row: P21 (23, 26, 29, 32) (34, 37, 40, 43), PM for side, p42 (48, 54, 58, 64) (70, 76, 80, 86), PM for side, p to end.

Work in St St until body measures approx 2.25 (2.75, 3.5, 3.75, 4.75) (5.25, 5.5, 6, 6.5)" / 6 (7, 9, 9, 12) (13, 14, 15, 16) cm from underarm or 0.75 (0.75, 0.75, 0.75, 0.75) (0.75, 1, 1, 1)" / 2 (2, 2, 2, 2) (2, 2.5, 2.5, 2.5) cm less than desired length to start of lower hem ending with a WS row.

WORK LOWER BACK SHAPING

Short Row 1 (RS): K to first m, SM, k to next m, SM, k3 (3, 3, 3, 3) (5, 5, 5, 6), turn.
Short Row 2 (WS): MDS, p to first m, SM, p to next m, SM, p3 (3, 3, 3, 3) (5, 5, 5, 6), turn.
Short Row 3 (RS): MDS, slipping all m's, k to 4 (4, 4, 4, 4) (7, 7, 7, 8) sts bef the DS, turn.
Short Row 4 (WS): MDS, p to 4 (4, 4, 4, 4) (7, 7, 7, 8) sts bef the DS, turn.
Rep short rows 3 and 4, 0 (0, 0, 0, 1) (1, 1, 2, 2) more time(s).

Next Row (RS): MDS, k to end, working the DSs as one (like a k2tog). [84 (94, 106, 116, 128) (138, 150, 160, 172) sts]
Next Row (WS): K, inc 1 st at centre back using an m1l, and at same time, work the rem DSs as one (like a k2tog). [85 (95, 107, 117, 129) (139, 151, 161, 173) sts]

LOWER HEM

With US 5 / 3.75 mm 24" / 60 cm circular needles and work as foll:
Row 1: *K1, p1* to last st, k1.
Row 2: P1, *k1, p1* to end.
Rep rows 1–2, 2 (2, 2, 2, 2) (2, 3, 3, 3) more times.
BO evenly in rib patt.

SLEEVES

Pl 33 (35, 40, 42, 45) (49, 52, 54, 56) sts on waste yarn for right sleeve onto US 6 / 4 mm needles, and beg at centre of underarm, pick up and k 1 (1, 2, 2, 2) (2, 3, 3, 3) st(s) along underarm CO sts, k34 (34, 38, 42, 46) (50, 54, 54, 58) sts from sleeve, and then pick up and k 2 (2, 2, 2, 3) (3, 3, 3, 3) sts along underarm CO to centre. PM for BOR. [36 (38, 44, 46, 50) (54, 58, 60, 62) sts]

Work 7 (5, 4, 8, 7) (9, 6, 9, 9) rnds in St St.
Dec Rnd: K1, ssk, k to last 3 sts, k2tog, k1. (2 sts dec'd)
Rep dec rnd every 10th (8th, 8th, 8th, 8th) (8th, 8th, 8th, 8th) rnd 2 (3, 4, 3, 2) (4, 3, 7, 8) more times, then every 0 (0, 0, 6th, 6th) (6th, 6th, 6th, 6th) rnd 0 (0, 0, 2, 4) (3, 6, 2, 2) more time(s). [30 (30, 34, 34, 36) (38, 38, 40, 40) sts]

If necessary, work even in St St in the rnd until sleeve measures 5 (5.25, 6.25, 7.25, 7.75) (9.25, 10.5, 12, 13)" / 13 (13, 16, 18, 19) (23, 26, 30, 33) cm or 0.75 (0.75, 0.75, 0.75, 0.75) (0.75, 1, 1, 1)" / 2 (2, 2, 2, 2) (2, 2.5, 2.5, 2.5) cm less than desired length to start of sleeve cuff.
Next Rnd: P.

SLEEVE CUFF

With US 5 / 3.75 mm set of DPNs, work as foll:
Rnd 1: *K1, p1* to end.
Cont in est 1 x 1 rib for 5 (5, 5, 5) (5, 7, 7, 7) more rnds.
BO evenly in 1 x 1 rib patt.
Work second sleeve as first.

BUTTON BANDS

LEFT FRONT BUTTON BAND

With RS facing and using US 5 / 3.75 mm 24" / 60 cm circular needles, pick up and k 42 (50, 52, 58, 66) (70, 74, 80, 86) sts evenly down left front edge (approx. 3 sts for every 4 rows).

Row 1: *K1, p1* to end.
Cont in est 1 x 1 rib for 4 (4, 4, 4, 4) (4, 6, 6, 6) more rows.
BO evenly in 1 x 1 rib patt.

RIGHT FRONT BUTTONHOLE BAND

Sizes 0–3 mos, 3–6 mos, 6–12 mos, 12–18 mos, 2 yr and 4 yr only
With RS facing and using US 5 / 3.75 mm 24" / 60 cm circular needles, pick up and k sts as bef, evenly up right front edge. [42 (50, 52, 58, 66) (70, –, –, –) sts]
Row 1: *K1, p1* to end.
Rep row 1 once more.
Next Row (make buttonholes): K1, p1, *k2tog, yo, (k1, p1) 3 (4, 3, 4, 4) (4, –, –, –) times*, rep *–* 3 (3, 4, 4, 5) (5, –, –, –) more times, k2tog, yo, *k1, p1* 3 (3, 4, 2, 1) (3, –, –, –) times.
Rep row 1, 2 more times.
BO evenly in 1 x 1 rib patt.

Sizes 6 yr, 8 yr, and 10 yr only
With RS facing and using US 5 / 3.75 mm 24" / 60 cm circular needles, pick up and k sts as bef, evenly up right front edge. [– (–, –, –, –) (–, 74, 80, 86) sts]
Row 1: *K1, p1* to end.
Rep row 1, 2 more times.

Next Row (make buttonholes): *K1, p1* – (–, –, –, –) (–, 5, 2, 5) times, *k2tog, yo, (k1, p1) – (–, –, –, –) (–, 4, 5, 5) times*, rep *–* – (–, –, –, –) (–, 5, 5, 5) more times, k2tog, yo, k1, p1.
Rep row 1, 3 more times.
BO evenly in 1 x 1 rib patt.

FINISHING

Weave in ends, closing any gaps that remain at the underarms. Using embroidery needle and threads, complete the embroidery on each front and centre back of cardigan using the below diagrams as your guide. Sew buttons to correspond to buttonholes on left front button band. Block to measurements.

LEFT FRONT

All in one strand

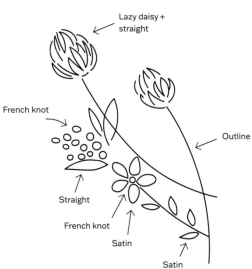

RIGHT FRONT

CENTRE BACK NECK

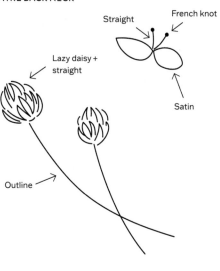

LANITA

I originally designed this pullover for an adult but couldn't help but imagine how cute the frilly cuffs would look on a child. Lanita can be knit in soft pastels or bold colours for a very different yet equally lovely result.

SIZES

6–12 mos (12–18 mos, 2 yr, 4 yr) (6 yr, 8 yr, 10 yr)
Recommended ease: 2–4″ / 5–10 cm of positive ease at chest

FINISHED MEASUREMENTS

Chest Circumference: 22.5 (24, 24.5, 26) (28.5, 29, 30.5)″ / 56 (60, 61, 65) (71, 73, 76) cm
Yoke Depth (front): 4.5 (4.75, 5, 6) (6.25, 6.75, 7)″ / 11.5 (12, 12.75, 15.25) (16, 17, 17.75) cm
Body Length Hem to Underarm (front): 5 (5.5, 6, 7.5) (9, 10, 11)″ / 13 (14, 15, 19) (23, 25, 28) cm
Upper Arm Circumference: 7.75 (8.5, 9, 9.75) (10, 10.5, 11.25)″ / 20 (21, 22, 24) (25, 26, 28) cm
Sleeve Length to Underarm: 6 (6.5, 7.5, 8.5) (10, 11.5, 12.5)″ / 15 (16, 19, 21) (25, 29, 31) cm

MATERIALS

Yarn:
Pink version shown in size 12–18 mos on Amanda (height 39″ / 97 cm)
Yarn A: 2 (2, 2, 2) (3, 3, 4) skeins of Silk Mohair by Isager (75% mohair, 25% silk, 231 yds / 212 m – 25 g), colourway 62
Or 267 (311, 352, 445) (553, 633, 727) yds / 244 (284, 321, 406) (505, 578, 664) m of lace-weight yarn

Yarn B: 1 (1, 2, 2) (2, 3, 3) skein(s) of Spinni by Isager (100% wool, 330 yds / 301 m – 50 g), colourway 61
Or 280 (327, 370, 467) (580, 664, 763) yds / 256 (299, 340, 427) (530, 607, 763) m of fingering-weight yarn

Blue version shown in size 4 yr on Anja (height 47″ / 120 cm)
Yarn A: 1 (2, 2, 2) (2, 3, 3) skein(s) of Silk Mohair by Isager 75% mohair, 25% silk, 231 yds / 212 m – 25 g), colourway 66
Or 319 (371, 420, 531) (659, 755, 867) yds / 291 (339, 384, 485) (602, 690, 792) m of lace-weight yarn

Yarn B: 2 (2, 3, 3) (4, 4, 5) skeins of Merino d'Arles by Rosy Green Wool (100% French organic merino d'arles, 218 yds / 200 m – 50 g), colourway Rivière
Or 350 (408, 462, 584) (725, 830, 954) yds / 320 (373, 422, 534) (662, 758, 872) m of fingering-weight yarn

Both yarns are held together throughout the pattern with the exception of the edging.

Needles: US 3 / 3.25 mm 16″ / 40 cm circular needles. US 6 / 4 mm 16″ / 40 cm, 24″ / 60 cm circular needles and a set of DPNs for sleeves. Crochet hook, US D-3 / 3.25 mm for baby sizes only

Notions: Stitch markers (1 of a different colour for BOR), stitch holders or waste yarn, tapestry needle, 1 button and crochet hook for baby sizes only

GAUGE

21.5 sts x 29 rnds to 4″ / 10 cm on US 6 / 4 mm needles in St St with yarns A and B held together, after blocking

1 repeat of Sugar Scallop pattern to 1″ / 2.5 cm on US 3 / 3.25 mm needles with yarn B only, after blocking

STITCH PATTERNS

SUGAR SCALLOP PATT (WORKED OVER MULTIPLE OF 11 STS PLUS 2)
Row 1 (WS): P.
Row 2: K2, [k1 and sl back to LH needle. With RH needle, lift next 8 sts, one at a time over the st just knit and off the needle, yo twice, k the first st again, k2] to end. (6 sts dec per rep)
Row 3: K1, [p2tog, drop the first yo of previous row, (k1, p1, k1, p1) all in second yo, p1] to last st, k1. (1 st inc per rep)
Rows 4–8: K.

EYELET YOKE PATT (WORKED OVER 7 STS)
Rnd 1 (RS): *K5, yo, k2tog* to end.
Rnds 2–7: K.
Rnd 8: *K2, yo, k2tog, k3* to end.
Rnds 9–14: K.

NOTES

Sleeve instructions are written for DPNs. However, an alternate method of working small circumferences, such as Magic-Loop Method or short circular needles, can be used. As the yoke increases, change to longer circular needles when necessary. Sizes 6–12 mos to 2 yr have a button closure at back neck.

INSTRUCTIONS

The sweater is worked from the top down with circular yoke and raglan shaping. A small section of short rows is worked at the back of the neck and above bottom hem for improved fit. The yoke is decorated with an eyelet pattern. The slightly shorter sleeves start at the cuff with the same scallop edging as the body. They also have a small section of short rows on their lower half to create a sculpted silhouette. Finally, the sleeves are grafted onto the body.

BODY

NECK EDGE

Using US 3 / 3.25 mm 16" / 40 cm circular needles and one strand of B yarn, CO 123 (123, 134, 134) (134, 145, 145) sts using the Long-Tail CO Method, or your preferred method. Do not join in the rnd.

Working back and forth on circular needles, work Sugar Scallop Patt (See Stitch Patt), working the 11-st rep 11 (11, 12, 12) (12, 13, 13) times across, until 5 rows of pattern have been completed. [68 (68, 74, 74) (74, 80, 80) sts]

Note! At the end of row 2, you should have 57 (57, 62, 62) (62, 67, 67) sts. At the end of row 3, you should have 68 (68, 74, 74) (74, 80, 80) sts.

With one strand each of A and B yarns held together throughout, complete rows 6 to 8 of Sugar Scallop Patt.

Join in rnd. Pl BOR m (centre back neck). Cont working with both strands of yarn as follows:
K 1 rnd.
Change to US 6 / 4 mm 16" / 40 cm circular needle (DPNs, or Magic-Loop for 2 smallest sizes) and k 1 rnd.

WORK BACK YOKE SHORT ROWS
Short Row 1 (RS): K20 (20, 21, 21, 21, 22, 22), turn.
Short Row 2 (WS): MDS, p to BOR, SM, p20 (20, 21, 21, 21, 22, 22), turn.
Short Row 3 (RS): MDS, k to BOR, SM, k to 4 sts bef last DS, turn.
Short Row 4 (WS): MDS, p to BOR, SM, p to 4 sts bef last DS, turn.
Rep short rows 3 and 4 once more.

Next Short Row (RS): MDS, k to BOR m.
Next Rnd: K, working both legs of each DS as one st (like a k2tog). [68 (68, 74, 74) (74, 80, 80) sts]
Adjustment Rnd: K, inc 0 (4, 0, 2) (8, 2, 8) st(s) evenly spaced around. [68 (72, 74, 76) (82, 82, 88) sts]
Inc Rnd (Change to longer circular needle when necessary): M1l, *k2, m1l* to last 2 sts, k2. [102 (108, 111, 114) (123, 123, 132) sts]
K 3 (4, 4, 4) (5, 6, 7) rnds.
Inc Rnd: K1, m1l, *k3, m1l* to last 2 sts, k2. [136 (144, 148, 152) (164, 164, 176) sts]
K 3 (4, 4, 4) (5, 6, 7) rnds.
Inc Rnd: K2, m1l, *k4, m1l* to last 2 sts, k2. [170 (180, 185, 190) (205, 205, 220) sts]
K 1 rnd.

Sizes 6–12 mos, 12–18 mos, 6 yr, 8 yr and 10 yr only
Adjustment Rnd: K, inc 5 (2, –, –) (5, 5, 4) sts evenly spaced around. [175 (182, –, –) (210, 210, 224) sts]

Sizes 2 yr & 4 yr only
Adjustment Rnd: K dec – (–, 3, 1) (–, –, –) sts evenly spaced around. [– (–, 182, 189) (–, –, –) sts]

All sizes resume
BEG YOKE PATT (SEE NOTE FOR PLAIN VERSION AT END)
Work Eyelet Yoke Patt (see Stitch Patt), working the 7-st rep 25 (26, 26, 27) (30, 30, 32) times around, until 14 rnds have been completed.

Sizes 4 yr, 6 yr, 8 yr and 10 yr only
Rep rnds 1 to 6 of eyelet yoke pattern once more.

All sizes resume
Sizes 6–12 mos, 12–18 mos, 2 yr, 4 yr and 10 yr only
Adjustment Rnd: K, inc 1 (2, 2, 3) (–, –, 0) st(s) evenly spaced around. [176 (184, 184, 192) (–, –, 224) sts]

Sizes 6 yr and 8 yr only
Adjustment Rnd: K, dec 2 sts evenly spaced around. [208 sts]

All sizes resume
SET-UP RAGLAN
Set-Up Rnd: K26 (27, 27, 28) (31, 31, 33), PM, k1, PM, k34 (36, 36, 38) (40, 40, 44), PM, k1, PM, k52 (54, 54, 56) (62, 62, 66), PM, k1, PM, k34 (36, 36, 38) (40, 40, 44), PM, k1, PM, k to end. [176 (184, 184, 192) (208, 208, 224) sts]

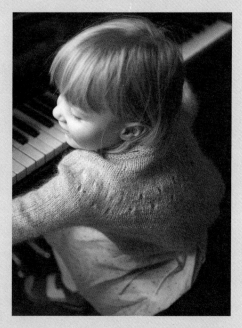

RAGLAN INCREASES

Inc Rnd: *K to next m, m1r, SM, k1, SM, m1l*, rep *–*
3 more times, k to end. (8 sts inc'd)
Next Rnd: K, slipping all m's.
Rep last 2 rnds 1 (1, 2, 2) (2, 3, 3) more time(s). [192 (200, 208, 216) (232, 240, 256) sts]

DIVIDE FOR BODY

Next Rnd: Leave BOR m in pl, k to next m, remove raglan ms as you come to them, sl next 38 (40, 42, 44) (46, 48, 52) sts for right sleeve onto waste yarn or holder, using Backwards Loop Method, CO 2 (4, 4, 6) (6, 6, 6) sts for right underarm placing a m in the centre of sts for side seam; k58 (60, 62, 64) (70, 72, 76) sts for front; sl next 38 (40, 42, 44) (46, 48, 52) sts for left sleeve onto waste yarn or holder, using Backwards Loop Method, CO 2 (4, 4, 6) (6, 6, 6) sts for left underarm placing a m in the centre of sts for side, k to BOR marker. [120 (128, 132, 140) (152, 156, 164) sts] (2 new m's placed with BOR at centre back)

Optional: For size 6–12 mos, change back to 16" / 40 cm circular needles if desired.

Work in St St in the rnd until body measures 3.5 (4, 4.5, 6) (7.5, 8.5, 9.5)" / 9 (10, 11, 15) (19, 21, 24) cm or 1.5" / 4 cm less than desired length from underarm to start of lower edge.

WORK BACK SHORT ROWS

Short Row 1 (RS): K to side m, SM, k8, turn.
Short Row 2 (WS): MDS, p to BOR, SM, p to side m, SM, p8, turn.
Short Row 3 (RS): MDS, k to BOR, SM, k to 4 sts bef DS, turn.
Short Row 4 (WS): MDS, p to BOR, SM, p to 4 sts bef DS, turn.
Rep short rows 3 and 4, 0 (0, 0, 0) (0, 1, 1) more time.

Next Short Row (RS): MDS, k to BOR m, SM, then k around, working DSs as one (like a k2tog) and removing side m's. [120 (128, 132, 140) (152, 156, 164) sts]

BOTTOM HEM

Rnd 1: *K1, p1* to end.
Work in est 1 x 1 rib for 8 more rnds.
BO evenly in rib.

SLEEVES

Using US 3 / 3.25 mm 16" / 40 cm circular needles and one strand of B yarn, CO 46 (57, 57, 68) (68, 79, 79) sts using the Long-Tail CO Method, or your preferred method. Do not join in the rnd.

Working back and forth on the circular needles, work Sugar Scallop Patt until 4 rows of patt have been completed. [26 (32, 32, 38) (38, 44, 44) sts]

Note! At the end of Row 2, you should have 22 (27, 27, 32) (32, 37, 37) sts. At the end of row 3, you should have 26 (32, 32, 38) (38, 44, 44) sts.

Join in rnd. Pl BOR m (centre of underarm).

P 1 rnd.

Change to US 6 / 4 mm DPNs or preferred needles for small circumference knitting. With one strand each of A and B yarns, begin working with both yarns held together throughout as foll:

Inc Rnd: K, inc 14 (12, 14, 12) (14, 10, 14) sts evenly spaced around. [40 (44, 46, 50) (52, 54, 58) sts]

WORK SHORT ROWS

Short Row 1 (RS): K14 (16, 16, 18) (18, 20, 22), turn.
Short Row 2 (WS): MDS, p to BOR, SM, p14 (16, 16, 18) (18, 20, 22), turn.
Short Row 3 (RS): MDS, k to BOR, SM, k to 4 sts bef DS, turn.
Short Row 4 (WS): MDS, p to BOR, SM, p to 4 sts bef DS, turn.
Rep short rows 3 and 4, 0 (0, 0, 1) (1, 2, 2) more time(s).

Next Short Row (RS): MDS, k to BOR m.
Next Rnd: K, working the DSs as one (like a k2tog). [40 (44, 46, 50) (52, 54, 58) sts]
Work in St St in the rnd until sleeve measures 5.5 (6, 7, 8) (9.5, 11, 12)" / 14 (15, 18, 20) (24, 28, 30) cm from just above the Sugar Scallop edging.

Next Rnd: K1, m1l, k to last st, m1r, k1. [42 (46, 48, 52) (54, 56, 60) sts]

Note! These extra 2 sts help hide any gaps when grafting sleeve to the sleeve sts left on waste yarn at end of yoke.

K 4 rnds even or work to desired length from cuff to underarm. Do not remove BOR m. Set aside, pl sts along with BOR m onto waste yarn or spare needle for grafting.

Work second sleeve as first.

FINISHING

Pl 38 (40, 42, 44) (46, 48, 52) sts left on waste yarn at yoke for right sleeve onto a spare needle. Pl the 42 (46, 48, 52) (54, 56, 60) sts of one sleeve onto another spare needle. Matching centre of the 2 (4, 4, 6) (6, 6, 6) underarm sts of body to centre (BOR m) of one sleeve, graft the sleeve sts to the yoke sts, rem m as you work. Ease in the extra 2 sleeve sts to help hide any gaps at the underarm and any yarn ends to close any gaps that remain. Rep for second sleeve.

Note! When grafting centre underarm sts of the sleeve to the body, you will not be grafting "live" sts to "live" sts as usual, but will be grafting "live sts" to CO sts.

Tack tog the beg and end of Sugar Scallop Edgings at sleeve cuffs if desired. Tack tog at centre back of neck for larger sizes only. Weave in ends and block to measurements.

Sizes 6–12 mos, 12–18 mos and 2 yr only
Starting at right neck edge, join one strand of B yarn and make a chain loop for buttonhole. Work 1 row of single crochet around back neck opening. Cut yarn and pull end through loop. Tighten and secure. Sew button on opposite side.

NIKOLETA

I have made this scarf countless times. It is a fun knit
that combines basic techniques and fine lace to create
a balanced, timeless piece. Work longer or shorter
depending on the size of your little one, or turn into
a cowl for a more modern look!

SIZE

One Size

FINISHED MEASUREMENTS

Length: 65.5" / 166 cm
Width: 11" / 28 cm

MATERIALS

Yarn:
Yarn A: 2 skeins of Merino by Knitting for Olive (100% merino wool, 273 yds / 249 m – 50 g), colourway Brown Nougat (pink version) and Pomegranate (red version)
Or 492 yds / 450 m of fingering-weight yarn

Yarn B: 2 skeins of Soft Silk Mohair by Knitting for Olive (70% mohair, 30% silk, 246 yds / 225 m – 25 g), colourway Brown Nougat (pink version) and Pomegranate (red version)
Or 492 yds / 450 m of lace-weight yarn

Both yarns are held together throughout the pattern

Needles: One pair of US 7 / 4.5 mm needles, or optional 24" / 60 cm circular needles

Notions: Stitch markers, cable needle, tapestry needle

GAUGE

20 sts x 26 rows to 4" / 10 cm on US 7 / 4.5 mm needles in St St with yarns A and B held together, after blocking.

19.5 sts x 25 rows to 4" / 10 cm on US 7 / 4.5 mm needles in Lace and Cable Patt with yarns A and B held together, after blocking.

SPECIAL ABBREVIATIONS

Sl1, k2tog, psso (double decrease): Sl 1 st, kwise, from the LHN to the RHN. K the next 2 sts on the LHN tog (k2tog), then using the left needle tip, lift the slipped st up and over the k2tog, and off the right needle tip

2/2 LC (2/2 Left Cross): Sl next 2 sts to CN and hold in front of work. K2, then k2 from CN

STITCH PATTERN

BROKEN SEED STITCH PATT (WORKED OVER 16 STS)
Row 1: K.
Row 2: P.
Rows 3–8: As rows 1 and 2.
Row 9: *K1, p1* to end.
Row 10: *P1, k1* to end.
Rep rows 1–10 for patt.

NOTES

When working with a double strand of yarn, it is easier to work from two separate skeins of yarn simultaneously. However, it might be necessary to split your last skein of yarn into two balls.

The chart is read from bottom to top and from right to left on RS rows and from left to right on WS rows.

INSTRUCTIONS

The scarf is worked flat with 2 strands of yarn. It is made up of 2 main panels: a broken seed stitch panel and a lace panel that is edged with a four-stitch cable twist.

Using US 7 / 4.5 mm needles and 1 strand of each yarn A and B held together throughout, CO 54 sts using the Long-Tail CO Method, or your preferred method.

Row 1 (RS): *K2, p2* to last 2 sts, k2.
Row 2 (WS): P2, *k2, p2* to end.
Work in 2 x 2 rib as est until work measures approx. 1.5" / 4 cm from CO edge, ending with a row 2 of rib patt and inc 1 st at centre of last row, using an m1l. [55 sts]

Beg body of scarf as folls:
Row 1 (RS): Sl1, PM, work row 1 of Broken Seed Stitch Patt over next 16 sts, PM, reading RS rows from right to left and WS rows from left to right, work row 1 of Chart over last 38 sts as foll: Work first 5 sts as indicated on chart, work 8-st rep 3 times, work last 9 sts as indicated on chart.
Row 2 (WS): Work row 2 of chart over first 38 sts as foll: Work first 9 sts as indicated on chart, work 8-st rep 3 times, work last 5 sts as indicated on chart, SM, work row 2 of Broken Seed Stitch Patt over next 16 sts, SM, p1.

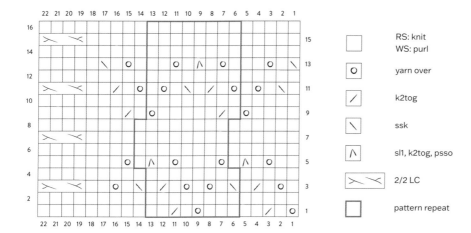

Chart legend:

□	RS: knit / WS: purl
O	yarn over
/	k2tog
\	ssk
∧	sl1, k2tog, psso
⤫	2/2 LC
□	pattern repeat

Cont in this manner as est, that is working appropriate rows of Broken Seed Stitch Patt and appropriate rows of chart, and at same time, rep rows 1–10 of Broken Seed Stitch Patt and rows 1-16 of chart until the chart has been worked a total of 24 times.

Cont in patts as est until a further 14 rows of chart have been completed and dec 1 st at centre of last row. Work should measure approx. 64" / 162.5 cm from CO edge. Alternatively, work until desired length, ending with a Row 14 of chart and dec 1 st at centre of last row. [54 sts]

Next Row (RS): *K2, p2* to last 2 sts, k2.
Next Row (WS): P2, *k2, p2* to end.
Work in 2 x 2 rib as est until work measures approx. 1.5" / 4 cm, ending with a WS row.
BO evenly in 2 x 2 rib patt as est.

FINISHING

Weave in ends and block to measurements.

WRITTEN INSTRUCTIONS FOR CHART

LACE AND CABLE PATT (WORKED FLAT OVER 38 STS AND 16 ROWS)
Row 1 (RS): Yo, k1, k2tog, k2, *k3, yo, k1, k2tog, k2* 3 times, k9.
Row 2 and all even rnds: P.
Row 3: K1, yo, k1, k2tog, k1, *ssk, k1, (yo, k1) twice, k2tog, k1* 3 times, ssk, k1, yo, k2, 2/2 LC.
Row 5: K2, yo, k1, sl1, k2tog, psso, k1, *yo, k3, yo, k1, sl1, k2tog, psso, k1* 3 times, yo, k7.
Row 7: K34, 2/2 LC.
Row 9: K4, yo, *k1, k2tog, k5, yo* 3 times, k1, k2tog, k7.
Row 11: K1, ssk, k1, yo, k1, *yo, k1, k2tog, k1, ssk, k1, yo, k1* 3 times, yo, k1, k2tog, k2, 2/2 LC.
Row 13: Ssk, k1, yo, k2, *k1, yo, k1, sl1, k2tog, psso, k1, yo, k2* 3 times, k1, yo, k1, ssk, k5.
Row 15: As row 7.

my fingers are
too fast for jazz!

PANDA

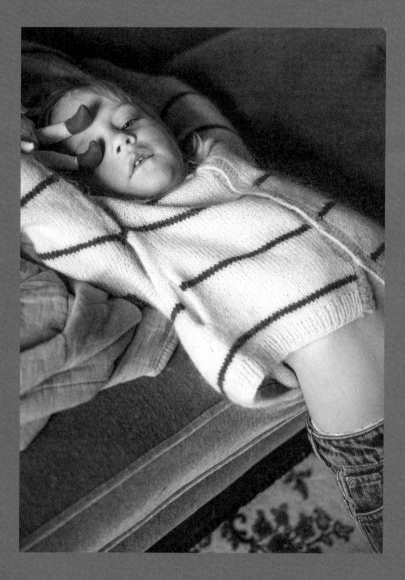

As a child, I loved collecting shells and shiny things from the beach, but not many of my garments had pockets to store my treasures. This memory inspired me to add pockets to this simple design that reminds me of cute panda bears. Make it as a cardigan or a sweater!

CARDIGAN

SIZES

0–3 mos (3–6 mos, 6–12 mos, 12–18 mos, 2 yr) (4 yr, 6 yr, 8 yr, 10 yr)
Recommended ease: 2" / 5 cm of positive ease at chest
Shown in size 4 yr on Amanda (height 38" / 97 cm)

FINISHED MEASUREMENTS

Chest Circumference: 14.5 (16.25, 18.5, 20.25, 22.5) (24.25, 26.25, 28.25, 30)" / 36 (41, 46, 51, 56) (61, 65, 71, 75) cm
Body Length to Underarm (front): 4.25 (4.75, 5.25, 5.75, 6.25) (7.75, 9.5, 10.5, 11.5)" / 8 (9, 11, 12, 13) (17, 20, 23, 25) cm
Raglan Depth: 3.75 (4, 4.5, 5, 5) (5.75, 6.25, 6.75, 7)" / 9 (10, 11, 13, 13) (15, 15, 17, 17) cm
Upper Arm Circumference: 6.25 (6.75, 7.5, 8.25, 9) (9.75, 10.25, 10.75, 11.5)" / 16 (17, 19, 20, 22) (24, 26, 27, 29) cm
Sleeve Length to Underarm: 5.75 (6, 7, 8, 8.5) (9.75, 11.5, 13, 14)" / 15 (15, 18, 20, 22) (25, 29, 33, 36) cm

MATERIALS

Yarn:
Yarn A: 1 (1, 1, 2, 2) (2, 2, 3, 3) skein(s) of Merino by Knitting for Olive (100% merino wool, 273 yds / 249 m – 50 g), colourway Putty
Or 164 (184, 237, 293, 344) (445, 545, 654, 760) yds / 150 (169, 217, 268, 315) (407, 499, 599, 695) m of fingering-weight yarn

Yarn B: 1 (1, 1, 2, 2) (2, 3, 3, 4) skein(s) of Soft Silk Mohair by Knitting for Olive (70% mohair, 30% silk, 246 yds / 225 m – 25 g), colourway Putty
Or 164 (184, 237, 293, 344) (445, 545, 654, 760) yds / 150 (169, 217, 268, 315) (407, 499, 599, 695) m lace-weight yarn

Yarn C: 1 (1, 1, 1, 1) (1, 1, 1, 1) skein of Merino by Knitting for Olive (100% merino wool, 273 yds / 249 m – 50 g), colourway Deep Petroleum Blue
Or 28 (27, 30, 37, 35) (41, 55, 60, 64) yds / 26 (25, 28, 34, 33) (38, 51, 55, 59) m of fingering-weight yarn

Yarn D: 1 (1, 1, 1, 1) (1, 1, 1, 1) skein of Soft Silk Mohair by Knitting for Olive (70% mohair, 30% silk, 246 yds / 225 m – 25 g), colourway Deep Petroleum Blue
Or 28 (27, 30, 37, 35) (41, 55, 60, 64) yds / 26 (25, 28, 34, 33) (38, 51, 55, 59) m of lace-weight yarn

1 strand of each yarn A and B are held together throughout the pattern for the Main Colour (MC).
1 strand of each yarn C and D are held together throughout the pattern for the Contrast Colour (CC).

Needles: US 3 / 3.25 mm 16" / 40 cm circular needles (optional), 24" / 60 cm and a set of DPNs. US 6 / 4 mm 16" / 40 cm circular needles (optional), 24" / 60 cm and a set of DPNs

Notions: Stitch markers, waste yarn or stitch holders, tapestry needle, 5 (6, 6, 6, 6) (7, 7, 7, 7) small buttons

GAUGE

22 sts x 30 rows to 4" / 10 cm on US 6 / 4 mm needles in St St, after blocking

STITCH PATTERN

STRIPE PATTERN
With 1 strand of each yarn C and D held together throughout (CC), work 2 rows in St St. With 1 strand of each yarn A and B held together throughout (MC), work 12 (14, 16, 16, 20) (22, 20, 22, 24) rows in St St, rep *–* for Stripe Patt.

NOTES

Sleeve instructions are written for a set of DPNs. However, an alternate method of working small circumferences, such as Magic-Loop Method or short circular needles, can be used for the larger sizes.
As the raglan shaping increases, change to longer circular needles when necessary.

INSTRUCTIONS

The cardigan is worked from the top down with raglan shaping. A small section of short rows is worked at the back of the neck for a more comfortable fit. Pocket linings are picked up around the pocket openings.

BODY

NECKBAND
With US 3 / 3.25 mm 24" / 60 cm circular needles and one strand of each yarn A and B held together throughout (MC), CO 54 (58, 62, 66, 70) (74, 78, 84, 88) sts using the Long-Tail CO Method, or your preferred method. You will continue to work flat.

Row 1 (RS): P.
Row 2 (WS): K.
Rep rows 1 and 2 once more.

Next Row (Adjustment Row): P, inc 6 (8, 8, 6, 6) (12, 10, 12, 10) sts evenly across, using an m1p. [60 (66, 70, 72, 76) (86, 88, 96, 98) sts]

Change to US / 4 mm 24" / 60 cm circular needles.
Set-Up Row (WS): P9 (10, 11, 12, 13) (14, 15, 17, 17) for right front, PM, p1, PM, p10 (10, 10, 10, 10) (12, 12, 12, 12) for right sleeve, PM, p1, PM, p18 (22, 24, 24, 26) (30, 30, 34, 36) for back, PM, p1, PM, p10 (10, 10, 10, 10) (12, 12, 12, 12) for left sleeve, PM, p1, PM, p9 (10, 11, 12, 13) (14, 15, 17, 17) for left front. [60 (66, 70, 72, 76) (86, 88, 96, 98) sts] (8 new m's placed for raglan)

WORK BACK NECK SHAPING
Note! You will be working back and forth while inc for the raglan at the same time as working short row shaping.

Short Row 1 (RS): *K to next m, m1r, SM, k1, SM, m1l*, rep *-* twice more, k5 (5, 5, 5, 5) (6, 6, 6, 6), turn. (6 sts inc'd)
Short Row 2 (WS): MDS, *p to next m, SM, p1, SM*, rep *-* once more, p5 (5, 5, 5, 5) (6, 6, 6, 6), turn.
Short Row 3 (RS): MDS, k to next m, m1r, SM, k1, SM, m1l, k to 2 sts bef m, turn. (2 sts inc'd)
Short Row 4 (WS): MDS, p to 2 sts from next m, turn.
Short Row 5 (RS): MDS, k to 2 (2, 2, 2, 2) (3, 3, 3, 4) sts bef the DS, turn.
Short Row 6 (WS): MDS, p to 2 (2, 2, 2, 2) (3, 3, 3, 4) sts bef the DS, turn.

Next Row (Inc): MDS, *k to next m working the DSs as one (like a k2tog), m1r, SM, k1, SM, m1l*, rep *-* once more, k to end. (4 sts inc'd)
Next Row (WS): MDS, slipping all m's, p to end of row, working the rem DSs as one (like a p2tog). [72 (78, 82, 84, 88) (98, 100, 108, 110) sts]

RAGLAN INCREASES
Row 1 (Inc): *K to next m, m1r, SM, k1, SM, m1l*, rep *-* 3 more times, k to end. (8 sts inc'd)
Row 2: *P to next m, SM, p1, SM*, rep *-* 3 more times, p to end.
Rep rows 1 and 2, 3 (3, 5, 5, 7) (8, 7, 8, 9) more times ending with a row 2. [104 (110, 130, 132, 152) (170, 164, 180, 190) sts]

BEG STRIPE PATT
Beg working in Stripe Patt throughout (see Stitch Pattern), and at same time cont to work raglan inc as est 1 (0, 0, 2, 4) (2, 6, 3, 5) more time(s). [112 (110, 130, 148, 184) (186, 212, 204, 230) sts]

Next Row (Inc): *K to next m, m1r, SM, k1, SM, m1l*, rep *-* 3 more times, k to end. (8 sts inc'd)
Next Row: *P to next m, SM, p1, SM*, rep *-* 3 more times, p to end.
Next Row: *K to next m, SM, k1, SM*, rep *-* 3 more times, k to end.
Next Row: *P to next m, SM, p1, SM*, rep *-* 3 more times, p to end.
Rep last 4 rows 2 (3, 3, 3, 1) (3, 2, 4, 3) more time(s).
Rep the first two rows once more (8 sts inc). [144 (150, 170, 188, 208) (226, 244, 252, 270) sts in total: 19 (20, 23, 26, 29) (31, 34, 36, 38) sts for each front, 31 (31, 35, 39, 43) (47, 51, 51, 55) sts for each sleeve and 40 (44, 50, 54, 60) (66, 70, 74, 80) sts for back and 4 raglan sts].

DIVIDE FOR BODY
Next Row (RS): Working in Stripe Patt as est, k to next m, removing all m's, pl next 33 (33, 37, 41, 45) (49, 53, 53, 57) sts (from left sleeve and 2 raglan sts) on to waste yarn, using Backwards Loop Method, CO 2 (4, 4, 4, 4) (4, 4, 6, 6) sts for left underarm, k across next 40 (44, 50, 54, 60) (66, 70, 74, 80) sts for back, pl next 33 (33, 37, 41, 45) (49, 53, 53, 57) sts (from right sleeve and 2 raglan sts) on to waste yarn, using Backwards Loop Method, CO 2 (4, 4, 4, 4) (4, 4, 6, 6) sts for right underarm, k to end. [80 (90, 102, 112, 124) (134, 144, 156, 166) sts]

Next Row: P19 (21, 24, 27, 30)(32, 35, 38, 40), PM for side, p42 (48, 54, 58, 64) (70, 74, 80, 86), PM for side, p to end.

Cont in St St and at same time, work in Stripe Patt as est until body measures approx 1 (1, 1.25, 1.25, 1.75) (2.75, 3, 3.5, 4)" / 3 (3, 4, 4, 5) (7, 8, 9, 10) cm from underarm ending with a p row.

POCKET OPENINGS

Cont to work Stripe Patt as est and at same time, beg opening for pockets as foll:

Next Row (RS): K to first m, RM, turn. Leave rem 61 (69, 78, 85, 94) (102, 109, 118, 126) sts on waste yarn or st holder.

Working back and forth on the next 20 (22, 25, 28, 31) (33, 36, 39, 41) sts, work 10 (10, 10, 18, 180 (18, 22, 22, 26) rows in St St. WS is facing for next row. Leave these sts on waste yarn or st holder.

With RS of work facing, join yarn to next 61 (69, 78, 85, 94) (102, 109, 118, 126) sts, k to m, RM, turn. Leave rem 20 (22, 25, 28, 31) (33, 36, 39, 41) sts on waste yarn or st holder.

Working back and forth on the 42 (48, 54, 58, 64) (70, 74, 80, 86) sts, work 10 (10, 10, 18, 18) (18, 22, 22, 26) rows in St St. WS is facing for next row. Leave these sts on waste yarn or st holder.

With RS of work facing, join yarn to rem 20 (22, 25, 28, 31) (33, 36, 39, 41) sts, work 11 (11, 11, 19, 19) (19, 23, 23, 27) rows in St St. WS is facing for next row.

Next Row: P20 (22, 25, 28, 31) (33, 36, 39, 41), p across 42 (48, 54, 58, 64) (70, 74, 80, 86) sts from waste yarn for back, p across rem 20 (22, 25, 28, 31) (33, 36, 39, 41) sts from waste yarn for left front. [82 (92, 104, 114, 126) (136, 146, 158, 168) sts]

Cont in St St and at same time, work in Stripe Patt as est until body measures approx 3.25 (3.75, 4.25, 4.75, 5.25) (6.75, 8, 9, 10)" / 8.25 (9.5, 10.75, 12, 13.25) (17, 20.25, 23, 25.5) cm from underarm or 0.75 (0.75, 0.75, 0.75, 0.75) (0.75, 1, 1, 1)" / 2 (2, 2, 2, 2) (2, 2.5, 2.5, 2.5) cm less than desired length to start of lower hem ending with a WS row.

Next Row: K, inc 1 st at centre back using an m1l. [83 (93, 105, 115, 127) (137, 147, 159, 169) sts]

LOWER HEM

With US 3 / 3.25 mm 24" / 60 cm circular needles and MC, work as foll:

Row 1: *K1, p1* to last st, k1.

Row 2: P1, *k1, p1* to end. Rep rows 1 and 2, 2 (2, 2, 2, 2) (2, 3, 3, 3) more times.

BO evenly in rib patt as est.

SLEEVES

Pl 33 (33, 37, 41, 45) (49, 53, 53, 57) sts on waste yarn for right sleeve onto US 6 / 4 mm set of DPNs or preferred style for working small circumferences. Beg at centre of underarm and working in Stripe Patt as est, pick up and k 1 (2, 2, 2, 2) (2, 2, 3, 3) st(s) along underarm CO sts, k 33 (33, 37, 41, 45) (49, 53, 53, 57) sts from sleeve, and then pick up and k 1 (2, 2, 2, 2) (2, 2, 3, 3) st(s) along underarm CO to centre. PM for BOR. [35 (37, 41, 45, 49) (53, 57, 59, 63) sts]

Beg with the appropriate row of Stripe Patt, work 12 (12, 10, 10, 6) (6, 6, 6, 6) rnds in St St.

Dec Rnd: K1, ssk, k to last 3 sts, k2tog, k1. (2 sts dec'd) Working in Stripe Patt as est, rep dec rnd every 12th (12th, 8th, 8th, 8th) (8th, 8th, 8th, 8th) rnd 1 (1, 3, 4, 2) (5, 6, 8, 9) more time(s), then every 6th rnd 0 (0, 0, 0, 4) (2, 2, 1, 1) more time(s). [31 (33, 33, 35, 35) (37, 39, 39, 41) sts]

If necessary, work in Stripe Patt as est until sleeve measures 5 (5.25, 6.25, 7.25, 7.75) (9, 10.5, 12, 13)" / 12.75 (13.25, 16, 18.5, 19.5) (23, 26.5, 30.5, 33) cm or 0.75 (0.75, 0.75, 0.75, 0.75) (0.75, 1, 1, 1)" / 2 (2, 2, 2, 2) (2, 2.5, 2.5, 2.5) cm less than desired length to start of sleeve cuff.

Next Rnd: K1, m1l, k to end. [32 (34, 34, 36, 36) (38, 40, 40, 42) sts]

SLEEVE CUFF

With US 3 / 3.25 mm set of DPNs or preferred style for working small circumferences and MC, work as foll:

Rnd 1: *K1, p1* to end.

Rep rnd 1, 5 (5, 5, 5, 5) (5, 7, 7, 7) more times.

BO evenly in 1 x 1 rib patt.

Work second sleeve as first.

POCKET LININGS

With RS facing, US 3 / 3.25 mm set of DPNs or preferred style for working small circumferences and MC, beg at lower opening of pocket, pick up and k 20 (20, 20, 36, 36) (36, 44, 44, 44) sts evenly around opening (approx. 1 st for every row). Evenly disperse sts over 4 DPNs. PM for BOR.

Work in St St in the rnd until pocket lining measures 1.5 (1.5, 2, 2.5, 3) (3, 3.5, 3.5, 4)" / 4 (4, 5.25, 6.5, 7.75) (7.75, 9, 9, 10) cm. RM. Leave these sts on waste yarn or st holder.

Work second pocket lining as first.

BUTTON BANDS

LEFT FRONT BUTTON BAND
With RS facing, US 3 / 3.25 mm 24" / 60 cm circular needles and MC, pick up and k 50 (56, 58, 68, 70) (82, 92, 102, 104) sts evenly down left front edge (approx. 3 sts for every 4 rows).

Row 1: *K1, p1* to end.
Rep row 1, 4 (4, 4, 4, 4) (4, 6, 6, 6) more times.
BO evenly in 1 x 1 rib patt.

RIGHT FRONT BUTTONHOLE BAND
Sizes 0-3 mos, 3-6 mos, 6–12 mos, 12–18 mos, 2 yr and 4 yr only
With RS facing and using US 3 / 3.25 mm 24" / 60 cm circular needles and MC, pick up and k sts as bef, evenly up right front edge and ending with same number of sts as for button band.

Row 1: *K1, p1* to end.
Rep row 1 once more.

Next Row (make buttonholes): K1, p1, *k2tog, yo, (k1, p1) 4 (4, 4, 5, 5) (5, –, –, –) times*, rep *–* 3 (4, 4, 4, 4) (5, –, –, –) more times, k2tog, yo, *k1, p1* 3 (1, 2, 2, 3) (3, –, –, –) time(s).

Rep row 1, 2 more times.
BO evenly in 1 x 1 rib patt.

Sizes 6 yr, 8 yr and 10 yr only
With RS facing and using US 3 / 3.25 mm 24" / 60 cm circular needles and MC, pick up and k sts as bef, evenly up right front edge and ending with same number of sts as for button band.

Row 1: *K1, p1* to end.
Rep row 1, 2 more times.

Next Row (make buttonholes): *K1, p1* – (–, –, –, –) (–, 2, 1, 2) time(s), *k2tog, yo, (k1, p1) – (–, –, –, –) (–, 6, 7, 7) times*, rep *–* – (–, –, –, –) (–, 5, 5, 5) more times, k2tog, yo, k1, p1.

Rep row 1, 3 more times.
BO evenly in 1 x 1 rib patt.

FINISHING

Weave in ends, closing any gaps that rem at the underarms. Use 3-Needle Bind-Off or Graft to join sts of pocket linings. Sew buttons to correspond to buttonholes on left front button band. Block to measurements.

SWEATER

SIZES

0–3 mos (3–6 mos, 6–12 mos, 12–18 mos, 2 yr) (4 yr, 6 yr, 8 yr, 10 yr)
Recommended ease: 2" / 5 cm of positive ease at chest
Shown in size 2 yr on Arvi (height 28" / 71 cm)

FINISHED MEASUREMENTS

Chest Circumference: 16 (17.75, 20, 21.75, 24) (25.75, 28, 29.75, 32)" / 40 (45, 50, 55, 60) (65, 70, 75, 80) cm
Body Length to Underarm (front): 4 (4.5, 5, 5.5, 6) (7.5, 9, 10, 11)" / 10 (11, 13, 14, 15) (19, 23, 26, 28) cm
Raglan Depth: 3.5 (3.25, 3.75, 4.5, 5.25) (5.25, 5.75, 5.55, 6.25)" / 9 (8, 10, 11, 13) (13, 15, 14, 16) cm
Upper Arm Circumference: 6.25 (6.75, 7.5, 8.25, 9) (9.75, 10.25, 10.75, 11.5)" / 16 (17, 19, 20, 22) (24, 26, 27, 29) cm
Sleeve Length to Underarm: 6.5 (6.75, 8.25, 9.75, 10.75) (12, 14, 15.5, 17)" / 17 (17, 21, 24, 27) (31, 36, 39, 43) cm

MATERIALS

Yarn:
Yarn A: 1 (1, 1, 2, 2) (2, 2, 3, 3) skein(s) of Merino by Knitting for Olive (100% merino wool, 273 yds / 249 m – 50 g), colourway Putty
Or 164 (184, 237, 293, 344) (445, 545, 654, 760) yds / 150 (169, 217, 268, 315) (407, 499, 599, 695) m of fingering-weight yarn

Yarn B: 1 (1, 1, 2, 2) (2, 3, 3, 4) skein(s) of Soft Silk Mohair by Knitting for Olive (70% mohair, 30% silk, 246 yds / 225 m – 25 g), colourway Putty
Or 164 (184, 237, 293, 344) (445, 545, 654, 760) yds / 150 (169, 217, 268, 315) (407, 499, 599, 695) m lace-weight yarn

Yarn C: 1 (1, 1, 1, 1) (1, 1, 1, 1) skein of Merino by Knitting for Olive (100% merino wool, 273 yds / 249 m – 50 g), colourway Deep Petroleum Blue
Or 28 (27, 30, 37, 35) (41, 55, 60, 64) yds / 26 (25, 28, 34, 33) (38, 51, 55, 59) m of fingering-weight yarn

Yarn D: 1 (1, 1, 1, 1) (1, 1, 1, 1) skein of Soft Silk Mohair by Knitting for Olive (70% mohair, 30% silk, 246 yds / 225 m – 25 g), colourway Deep Petroleum Blue

Or 28 (27, 30, 37, 35) (41, 55, 60, 64) yds / 26 (25, 28, 34, 33) (38, 51, 55, 59) m of lace-weight yarn

1 strand of each yarn A and B are held together throughout the patt for the Main Colour (MC). 1 strand of each yarn C and D are held together throughout the patt for the Contrast Colour (CC)

Needles: US 3 / 3.25 mm 16" / 40 cm circular needles, 24" / 60 cm, and a set of DPNs. US 6 / 4 mm 16" / 40 cm circular needles (optional), 24" / 60 cm, and a set of DPNs

Notions: Stitch markers, waste yarn or stitch holders, tapestry needle, 1 small button for baby sizes and 2 yr size only

GAUGE

22 sts x 30 rnds to 4" / 10 cm on US 6 / 4 mm needles in St St, after blocking

STITCH PATTERN

STRIPE PATTERN
*With 1 strand each of C and D held together throughout (CC), work 2 rnds St St.
With 1 strand each of A and B held together throughout (MC), work 12 (14, 16, 16, 20) (22, 20, 22, 24) rnds St St*, rep *–* for Stripe Patt.

NOTES

Sleeve instructions are written for a set of DPNs. However, an alternate method of working small circumferences, such as Magic-Loop Method or short circular needles, can be used for the larger sizes.
As the raglan shaping increases, change to longer circular needles when necessary.

INSTRUCTIONS

The pullover is worked from the top down with raglan shaping. A small section of short rows is worked at the back of the neck for a more comfortable fit. Pocket linings are picked up around the pocket openings.

BODY

NECK EDGE

Sizes 0–3 mos, 3–6 mos, 6–12 mos, 12–18 mos and 2 yr only

With US 3 / 3.25 mm 16" / 40 cm circular needles and one strand each of A and B held together throughout (MC), CO 66 (70, 72, 74, 76) (–, –, –, –) sts using the Long-Tail CO Method, or your preferred method. Do not join in the rnd.

Working back and forth on the circular needle, p 1 row.

Next Row: K2, yo, k2tog (buttonhole made), k to end.

Next Row: P.

Next Row (WS): BO 6 sts pwise for button tab, p to end, turn. RS is facing. Join in rnd. Pl BOR m (centre back neck). [60 (64, 66, 68, 70) (–, –, –, –) sts]

Sizes 4 yr, 6 yr, 8 yr and 10 yr only

With US 3 / 3.25 mm set of DPNs or 16" / 40 cm circular needles and one strand each of A and B held together throughout (MC), CO – (–, –, –, –) (74, 78, 82, 86) sts using the Long-Tail CO Method, or your preferred method. Join in the rnd making sure sts are not twisted. PM for BOR (centre back neck).

Rnd 1: P.

Rep rnd 1, 2 more times.

All sizes resume

Next Rnd (Adjustment Rnd): K, inc 6 (8, 10, 10, 12) (18, 18, 20, 20) sts evenly across, using an m1l. [66 (72, 76, 78, 82) (92, 96, 102, 106) sts]

Change to US 6 / 4 mm 24" / 60 cm circular needles.

Set-Up Rnd: K11 (12, 13, 14, 15) (16, 17, 19, 20) for right back, PM, k1, PM, k10 (10, 10, 10, 10) (12, 12, 12, 12) for right sleeve, PM, k1, PM, k20 (24, 26, 26, 28) (32, 34, 36, 38) for front, PM, k1, PM, k10 (10, 10, 10, 10) (12, 12, 12, 12) for left sleeve, PM, k1, PM, k11 (12, 13, 14, 15) (16, 17, 19, 20) for left back. [66 (72, 76, 78, 82) (92, 96, 102, 106) sts] (8 new m's placed)

BACK NECK SHAPING

Note! You will be working back and forth while inc for the raglan at the same time as working short row shaping.

Short Row 1 (RS): K to next m, m1r, SM, k1, SM, m1l, k5 (5, 5, 5, 5) (6, 6, 6, 6), turn. (2 sts inc'd)

Short Row 2 (WS): MDS, p to next m, SM, p1, SM, p to BOR, SM, p to next m, SM, p1, SM, p5 (5, 5, 5, 5) (6, 6, 6, 6), turn.

Short Row 3 (RS): MDS, k to next m, m1r, SM, k1, SM, m1l, k to BOR, SM, k to 2 sts from next m, turn. (2 sts inc'd)

Short Row 4 (WS): MDS, p to BOR, SM, p to 2 sts from next m, turn.

Short Row 5 (RS): MDS, slipping the BOR, k to 2 (2, 2, 2, 2) (3, 3, 3, 4) sts bef the DS, turn.

Short Row 6 (WS): MDS, slipping the BOR, p to 2 (2, 2, 2, 2) (3, 3, 3, 4) sts bef the DS, turn.

Next Row: MDS, k back to BOR.

Next Rnd: *K to next m, working the double sts as one (like a k2tog), m1r, SM, k1, SM, m1l*, rep *–* 3 more times, k to end working the rem DSs as one (like a k2tog). (8 sts inc'd) [78 (84, 88, 90, 94) (104, 108, 114, 118) sts]

Next Rnd: *K to next m, SM, k1, SM*, rep *–* 3 more times, k to end.

RAGLAN INCREASES

Rnd 1 (Inc): *K to next m, m1r, SM, k1, SM, m1l*, rep *–* 3 more times, k to end. (8 sts inc'd)

Rnd 2: *K to next m, SM, k1, SM*, rep *–* 3 more times, k to end.

Rep rnds 1 and 2, 3 (3, 5, 5, 7) (8, 7, 8, 9) more times ending with a rnd 2. [110 (116, 136, 138, 158) (176, 172, 186, 198) sts]

BEG STRIPE PATT

Beg working in Stripe Patt throughout (see Stitch Pattern), and at same time cont to work both raglan inc rnds as est 1 (0, 0, 2, 4) (2, 6, 3, 5) more time(s). [118 (116, 136, 154, 190) (192, 220, 210, 238) sts]

Rnd 1 (Inc): *K to next m, m1r, SM, k1, SM, m1l*, rep *–* 3 more times, k to end. (8 sts inc'd)

Rnd 2: *K to next m, SM, k1, SM*, rep *–* 3 more times, k to end.

Rnds 3–4: As rnd 2.

Rep last 4 rnds 2 (3, 3, 3, 1) (3, 2, 4, 3) more time(s).

Rep rnds 1 and 2 once more. [150 (156, 176, 194, 214, 232, 252, 258, 278) sts total: 40 (44, 50, 54, 60) (66, 72, 74, 80) sts for front, 44 (46, 52, 58, 64) (68, 74, 78, 84) sts for back, 33 (33, 37, 41, 45) (49, 53, 53, 57) sts for each sleeve with raglan sts].

DIVIDE FOR BODY

Next Row (RS): Leave BOR m in pl and, working in Stripe Patt as est, k to next m, RM and cont to remove m when come to it, pl next 33 (33, 37, 41, 45) (49, 53, 53, 57) sts for right sleeve on to waste yarn or holder, using Backwards Loop Method, CO 2 (4, 4, 4, 4) (4, 4, 6, 6) sts, k across next 40 (44, 50, 54, 60) (66, 72, 74, 80) sts for front, pl next 33 (33, 37, 41, 45) (49, 53, 53, 57) sts for left sleeve on to waste yarn or holder, using Backwards Loop Method, CO 2 (4, 4, 4, 4) (4, 4, 6, 6) sts, k to end. [88 (98, 110, 120, 132) (142, 154, 164, 176) sts]

Next Rnd: K23 (25, 28, 31, 34) (36, 39, 42, 45), PM for side, k42 (48, 54, 58, 64) (70, 76, 80, 86), PM for side, k to end.

Cont in St St in the rnd and at same time, work in Stripe Patt as est until body measures approx. 1 (1, 1.25, 1.25, 1.75) (2.75, 3, 3.5, 4)" / 3 (3, 3, 3, 4) (7, 8, 9, 10) cm from underarm.

POCKET OPENINGS

Cont to work Stripe Patt as est and at same time, beg opening for pockets as foll:

Next Row: K to first m, RM, turn. P to BOR, remove BOR, p to next m, turn. Leave rem 42 (48, 54, 58, 64) (70, 76, 80, 86) sts on waste yarn or st holder.

Working back and forth on the 46 (50, 56, 62, 68) (72, 78, 84, 90) sts, work 9 (9, 9, 17, 17) (17, 21, 21, 25) rows in St St. You will have ended on a k row. Leave these sts on waste yarn or st holder.

With RS of work facing, join yarn to rem 42 (48, 54, 58, 64) (70, 76, 80, 86) sts, k to m, RM, turn.

Working back and forth on the 42 (48, 54, 58, 64) (70, 76, 80, 86) sts, work 10 (10, 10, 18, 18) (18, 22, 22, 26) rows in St St. You will have ended on a k row.

Next Rnd: K across 23 (25, 28, 31, 34) (36, 39, 42, 45) sts from waste yarn for back, PM for BOR, k across rem 23 (25, 28, 31, 34) (36, 39, 42, 45) sts from waste yarn for back, k across front sts to BOR. [88 (98, 110, 120, 132) (142, 154, 164, 176) sts]

Cont in St St in the rnd and at same time, work in Stripe Patt as est until body measures approx. 3.25 (3.75, 4.25, 4.75, 5.25) (6.75, 8, 9, 10)" / 8 (9, 11, 12, 13) (17, 20, 23, 25) cm from underarm or 0.75 (0.75, 0.75, 0.75, 0.75) (0.75, 1, 1, 1)" / 2 (2, 2, 2, 2) (2, 3, 3, 3) cm less than desired length to start of lower hem.

LOWER HEM

With US 3 / 3.25 mm 24" / 60 cm circular needles and MC, work as foll:

Rnd 1: *K1, p1* to end.

Rep rnd 1, 5 (5, 5, 5, 5) (5, 7, 7, 7) more times.

BO evenly in 1 x 1 rib patt.

SLEEVES

Pl 33 (33, 37, 41, 45) (49, 53, 53, 57) sts on waste yarn for right sleeve onto US 6 / 4 mm set of DPNs or preferred style for working small circumferences. Beg at centre of underarm and working in Stripe Patt as est, pick up and k 1 (2, 2, 2, 2) (2, 2, 3, 3) sts along underarm CO sts, k 33 (33, 37, 41, 45) (49, 53, 53, 57) sts from sleeve, and then pick up and k 1 (2, 2, 2, 2) (2, 2, 3, 3) sts along underarm CO to centre. PM for BOR. [35 (37, 41, 45, 49) (53, 57, 59, 63) sts]

Beg with the appropriate row of Stripe Patt, work 12 (12, 10, 10, 6) (6, 6, 6, 6) rnds in St St.

Dec Rnd: K1, ssk, k to last 3 sts, k2tog, k1. (2 sts dec'd) Working in Stripe Patt as est, rep dec rnd every 12th (12th, 8th, 8th, 8th) (8th, 8th, 8th, 8th) rnd 1 (1, 3, 4, 2) (5, 6, 8, 9) more time(s), then every 6th rnd 0 (0, 0, 0, 4) (2, 2, 1, 1) more time(s). [31 (33, 33, 35, 35) (37, 39, 39, 41) sts]

If necessary, work in Stripe Patt as est until sleeve measures 5 (5.25, 6.25, 7.25, 7.75) (9, 10.5, 12, 13)" / 13 (13, 16, 18, 19) (23, 26, 30, 33) cm or 0.75 (0.75, 0.75, 0.75, 0.75) (0.75, 1, 1, 1)" / 2 (2, 2, 2, 2) (2, 3, 3, 3) cm less than desired length to start of sleeve cuff.

Next Rnd: K1, m1l, k to end. [32 (34, 34, 36, 36) (38, 40, 40, 42) sts]

SLEEVE CUFF
With US 3 / 3.25 mm set of DPNs or preferred style for working small circumferences and MC, work as foll:
Rnd 1: *K1, p1* to end.
Rep rnd 1, 5 (5, 5, 5, 5) (5, 7, 7, 7) more times.
BO evenly in 1 x 1 rib patt.
Work second sleeve as first.

POCKET LININGS

With RS facing, US 3 / 3.25 mm set of DPNs or preferred style for working small circumferences and MC, beg at lower opening of pocket, pick up and k 20 (20, 20, 36, 36) (36, 44, 44, 44) sts evenly around opening (approx. 1 st for every row). Evenly disperse sts over 4 DPNs. PM for BOR.

Work in St St in the rnd until pocket lining measures 1.5 (1.5, 2, 2.5, 3) (3, 3.5, 3.5, 4)" / 4 (4, 5, 6, 8) (8, 9, 9, 10) cm. RM. Leave these sts on waste yarn or st holder.

Work second pocket lining as first.

FINISHING

Weave in ends, closing any gaps that rem at the underarms. Use 3-Needle Bind-Off or Grafting to join sts of pocket linings. Sizes 0–3 mos, 3–6 mos, 6–12 mos, 12–18 mos and 2 yr sew button to correspond to buttonhole on neckband. Block to measurements.

TOGETHER APART

I designed the Together Apart sweater at the beginning of the COVID-19 pandemic. The parallel winding rows on the yoke represented togetherness at a time when we were physically apart.

SIZES

6–12 mos (12–18 mos, 2 yr, 4 yr) (6 yr, 8 yr, 10 yr)
Recommended ease: 2–4" / 5–10 cm of positive ease at chest

FINISHED MEASUREMENTS

Chest Circumference: 20.5 (22.5, 24, 25.5) (28, 29, 30.5)" / 51 (56, 60, 64) (70, 73, 76) cm
Yoke Depth (front): 4.75 (5, 4.5, 5.75) (5.5, 7, 7.25)" / 12 (13, 11, 14) (14, 18, 18) cm
Body Length to Underarm (front): 7.5 (8.5, 9, 10.5) (11.5, 13, 14)" / 19 (21, 23, 26) (29, 33, 35) cm
Upper Arm Circumference: 7 (7.5, 8, 9) (9.75, 10.75, 11)" / 18 (19, 20, 23) (24, 27, 28) cm
Sleeve Length to Underarm: 7.5 (8.5, 9, 10.5) (11.5, 13, 14)" / 19 (21, 23, 26) (29, 33, 35) cm

MATERIALS

Yarn:
Cream version shown in size 4 yr on Amanda (height 38" / 97 cm)
Yarn A: 1 (1, 1, 1) (1, 2, 2) skein(s) of Merino Singles by Qing Fibre (100% SW merino, 400 yds / 366 m – 100 g), colourway Champagne
Or 175 (210, 230, 290) (335, 405, 440) yds / 160 (192, 210, 265) (306, 370, 402) m of fingering-weight yarn

Yarn B: 1 (1, 1, 1) (1, 1, 1) skein of Kid Mohair Silk by Qing Fibre (70% ultrafine kid mohair, 30% silk, 459 yds / 420 m – 100 g), colourway Champagne
Or 175 (210, 230, 290) (335, 405, 440) yds / 160 (192, 210, 265) (306, 370, 402) m of lace-weight yarn

Teal version shown in size 4 yr on Anja (height 47" / 120 cm)
Yarn A: 1 (1, 1, 1) (1, 2, 2) skein(s) of Merino by Knitting for Olive (100% merino wool, 273 yds / 249 m – 50 g), colourway Dusty Dove Blue
Or 175 (210, 230, 290) (335, 405, 440) yds / 160 (192, 210, 265) (306, 370, 402) m of fingering-weight yarn

Yarn B: 1 (1, 1, 2) (2, 2, 2) skein(s) of Soft Silk Mohair by Knitting for Olive (70% mohair, 30% silk, 246 yds / 225 m – 25 g), colourway Dusty Dove Blue

Or 175 (210, 230, 290) (335, 405, 440) yds / 160 (192, 210, 265) (306, 370, 402) m of lace-weight yarn

Both yarns are held together throughout pattern.

Needles: US 8 / 5 mm 16" / 40 cm, 24" / 60 cm circular needles and a set of DPNs

Notions: Stitch markers (1 of a different colour for BOR), stitch holders or waste yarn, tapestry needle, 1 button for baby sizes only

GAUGE

18 sts x 27 rnds to 4" / 10 cm on US 8 / 5 mm needles in St St with yarns A and B held together, after blocking

NOTES

Sleeve instructions are written for DPNs. However, an alternate method of working small circumferences, such as Magic-Loop Method or short circular needles, can be used. As the yoke decreases, change to shorter circular needles or DPNs when necessary. Sizes 6–12 mos to 18 mos have a button closure at back neck and will require a button. Row gauge is important to obtain the correct yoke depth. Be sure to swatch!

Charts are read from bottom to top and from right to left when knitting in the rnd.

INSTRUCTIONS

The pullover is worked from the bottom up with circular yoke and raglan shaping. The body and sleeves are knit separately in the round to the base of the yoke, then joined. A section of short rows is worked at the back hem for a more comfortable fit.

SLEEVES

Using US 8 / 5 mm DPNs and a strand each of yarns A and B held together, CO 20 (22, 24, 26) (28, 30, 32) sts using the Long-Tail CO Method, or your preferred method. Join in the rnd making sure sts are not twisted. PM for BOR.

Rnd 1: *K1, p1* to end.

Work in 1 x 1 rib as est until work measures 1 (1, 1, 1.5) (1.5, 1.5, 1.5)" / 3 (3, 3, 4) (4, 4, 4) cm from CO edge. Change to St St in the rnd and k 3 (5, 5, 5) (5, 5, 7) rnds.

SLEEVE INCREASES

Inc Rnd: K1, m1l, k to 1 st bef BOR m, m1r, k1. (2 sts inc'd) Rep inc rnd every 4th (6th, 6th, -) (6th, -, 8th) rnd 1 (3, 2, -) (1, -, 6) more time(s), then every 6th (8th, 8th, 8th) (8th, 8th, 10th) rnd 4 (2, 3, 6) (6, 8, 2) more times. [32 (34, 36, 40) (44, 48, 50) sts]. 32 (40, 42, 54) (60, 70, 76) rnds worked after cuff.

Work in St St in the rnd until sleeve measures 7.5 (8.5, 9, 10.5) (11.5, 13, 14)" / 19 (21, 23, 26) (29, 33, 35) cm from CO edge, or desired length to underarm.

Next Rnd: K, ending 2 (2, 2, 3) (3, 3, 3) sts bef BOR m. Pl next 4 (4, 4, 6) (6, 6, 6) sts on waste yarn or st holder for underarm, removing m when you come to it.

Set aside first sleeve, pl rem 28 (30, 32, 34) (38, 42, 44) sts on waste yarn or spare needle.
Work second sleeve as first.

BODY

Using US 8 / 5 mm 16" / 40 cm (or longer for child sizes) circular needles, and a strand of yarns A and B held together, CO 92 (102, 108, 114) (126, 130, 138) sts using the Long-Tail CO Method, or your preferred method. Join in the rnd making sure sts are not twisted. PM for BOR.

Rnd 1: *K1, p1* to end.

Work in 1 x 1 rib as est until work measures 1 (1, 1, 1.5) (1.5, 1.5, 1.5)" / 3 (3, 3, 4) (4, 4, 4) cm from CO edge.

Next Rnd: K46 (51, 54, 57) (63, 65, 69), PM for side, k to end.

WORK BACK SHORT ROWS

Short Row 1 (RS): K to side m, SM, k6, w&t.
Short Row 2 (WS): P to BOR, sl BOR m, p6, w&t.
Short Row 3 (RS): K to 3 sts bef wrapped st, w&t.
Short Row 4 (WS): P to 3 sts bef wrapped st, w&t.
Rep short rows 3 and 4, 0 (0, 0, 1) (1, 1, 2) time(s) more.

Next Rnd (RS): K around, slipping side m and concealing wrapped sts as you come to them as foll: Sl the RHN under the wrap and k it tog with the st that it wraps. [92 (102, 108, 114) (126, 130, 138) sts]

Work in St St in the rnd until work measures 7.5 (8.5, 9, 10.5) (11.5, 13, 14)" / 19 (21, 23, 26) (29, 33, 35) cm from front CO edge or desired length to underarm and ending 2 (2, 2, 3) (3, 3, 3) sts bef BOR m.

JOIN FOR YOKE

Next Rnd: K next 4 (4, 4, 6) (6, 6, 6) sts, then pl these sts on waste yarn for right underarm, removing BOR m. K across back sts to 2 (2, 2, 3) (3, 3, 3) sts bef side m, PM, pl next 4 (4, 4, 6) (6, 6, 6) sts on waste yarn for underarm, RM. Transfer sts from first sleeve on to left needle of body, and k 28 (30, 32, 34) (38, 42, 44) sts for left sleeve, PM, then k across front sts to end, PM. Transfer sts from second sleeve on to left needle of body and k 28 (30, 32, 34) (38, 42, 44) sts for right sleeve. PM for new BOR (right back shoulder). [140 (154, 164, 170) (190, 202, 214) sts]

RAGLAN DECREASES

Dec Rnd: *K1, k2tog, k to 3 sts bef next m, ssk, k1, SM*. Rep *-* 3 more times. (8 sts dec'd)
Rep dec rnd every rnd 3 (3, 3, 3) (3, 4, 4) more times. [108 (122, 132, 138) (158, 162, 174) sts]

Adjustment Rnd: Dec 10 (10, 4, 10) (5, 9, 4) sts evenly spaced around. [98 (112, 128, 128) (153, 153, 170) sts]

K 1 (3, 0, 2) (0, 2, 4) rnd(s).

BEG YOKE PATT

Change to 16" / 40 cm circular needle or DPNs as necessary.

Beg working yoke patt from chart on row specified for your size, working the rep 7 (8, 8, 8) (9, 9, 10) times around, and working dec's where indicated until all rnds of chart are complete. [63 (72, 72, 72) (81, 81, 90) sts]

Adjustment Rnd: Dec 9 (14, 12, 10) (15, 13, 18) sts evenly spaced around. [54 (58, 60, 62) (66, 68, 72) sts]

it's a lullaby!

NECKBAND

Sizes 6–12 mos and 12–18 mos only
With US 8 / 5 mm 16" / 40 cm circular needles, begin working back and forth as folls:
Row 1 (WS): Turn work so that WS is facing, *k1, p1* to end, using Backwards Loop Method, CO 4 sts. [58 (62, –, –) (–, –, –) sts]
Row 2 (RS): K2, *p1, k1* to last 3 sts p1, k2.
Row 3 (WS): P2, *k1, p1* to last 3 sts, k1, p2.
Row 4 (make buttonhole): K2, yo, k2tog, *p1, k1* to last 3 sts, p1, k2.
Row 5: As Row 3.
Row 6: As Row 2.
BO loosely in 1 x 1 rib patt.

Sizes 2 yr, 4 yr, 6 yr, 8 yr and 10 yr only
Rnd 1: *K1, p1* to end.
Work in 1 x 1 rib as est until work measures 1" / 2.5 cm.
BO loosely in 1 x 1 rib patt.

FINISHING

Use 3-Needle Bind-Off on WS or Grafting to join underarm sts. Weave in ends, closing any gaps that remain at the underarms. For baby sizes, sew the button onto the neck band to correspond to the buttonhole. Block to measurements.

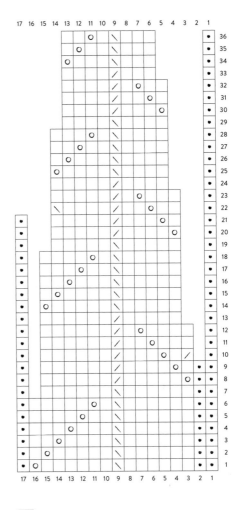

	knit
•	purl
/	k2tog
\	ssk
O	yo

Note! Sizes 6, 8 and 10 yrs begin on row 1.
Sizes 2 and 4 yrs begin on row 8.
Sizes 6–12 mos and 12–18 mos begin on row 14.

OSCAR

Oscar was inspired by my son, who was an energetic and adventurous child. As such, he always wanted his arms as uninhibited as possible, even on the chilliest of days. This modern take on a traditional vest is sure to keep your child's chest warm on colder days, while leaving the arms free.

SIZES

0–6 mos (6–12 mos, 12–18 mos, 2 yr) (4 yr, 6 yr, 8 yr, 10 yr)
Recommended ease: 2″ / 5 cm of positive ease

FINISHED MEASUREMENTS

Chest Circumference: 18 (20, 22, 24) (26, 28, 30, 32)″ /
46 (50, 55, 59) (65, 70, 74, 80 cm
Body Length to Underarm: 4.5 (5, 6, 7.5) (9, 10, 11, 11.5)″ /
11 (13, 15, 19) (23, 25, 28, 29) cm
Armhole Depth: 4 (4.5, 5, 5) (6, 6.25, 6.75, 7)″ / 10 (12, 12,
13) (15, 16, 17, 17) cm
Back Neck Width: 3.25 (4, 4, 4.75) (4.75, 4.75, 5.5, 6.25)″ /
8.25 (10, 10, 12) (12, 12, 14, 16) cm
Front Neck Depth: 1.5 (1.5, 1.75, 1.75) (2, 2, 2.25, 2.5)″ /
4 (4, 4, 4) (5, 5, 6, 6) cm

MATERIALS

Yarn:
*Light blue version shown in size 2 yr on Amanda
(height 38″ / 97 cm)*
1 (1, 1, 1) (2, 2, 2, 2) skein(s) of Jensen by Isager (100%
wool, 273 yds / 250 m – 100 g), colourway 11s

*Dark blue version shown in size 4 yr on Anja
(height 47″ / 120 cm)*
1 (1, 2, 2) (2, 3, 3, 3) skein(s) of Vovo by Retrosaria Rosa
Pomar (100% wool, 156 yds / 142 m – 50 g) colourway 03

Or 120 (145, 185, 235) (300, 350, 405, 450) yds / 108 (131,
169, 213) (272, 320, 368, 412) m of DK-weight yarn

Needles: US 2 / 2.75 mm 16″ / 40 cm circular needles
and a set of DPNs. US 4 / 3.5 mm 16″ / 40 cm circular
needles (for four smallest sizes), 24″ / 60 cm circular
needles (for sizes 4–10 yrs)

Notions: Stitch markers, waste yarn or stitch holders,
tapestry needle, 1 small button (for smallest 3 sizes)

GAUGE

21 sts x 34 rows to 4″ / 10 cm on US 4 / 3.5 mm needles
in St St, after blocking

21 sts x 34 rows to 4″ / 10 cm on US 4 / 3.5 mm needles
in Texture St, after blocking

NOTES

Neckband and armband instructions are written for a
set of DPNs. However, an alternate method of working
small circumferences, such as Magic-Loop Method or
short circular needles, can be used for the larger sizes.
Sizes 0–6 mos, 6–12 mos and 12–18 mos have a button
closure at back neck and will require a button.

INSTRUCTIONS

The vest is worked from the bottom up in the round,
then split into 2 pieces for the armhole shaping.
The shoulders are seamed after which the neckband
and armbands are picked up and worked in the round.
A button closure at the back of the neck is included
for the 3 smallest sizes.

BODY

BOTTOM HEM
With US 2 / 2.75 mm 16″ / 40 cm circular needles, CO 96
(104, 116, 124) (136, 148, 156, 168) sts using the Long-Tail
CO Method, or your preferred method. Join in the rnd
making sure sts are not twisted. PM for BOR.

Rnd 1: *K1, p1* to end.
Rep rnd 1, 5 more times.

Change to US 4 / 3.5 mm 16″ / 40 cm circular needles
for smaller sizes or 24″ / 60 cm circular needles for
larger sizes.

Rnd 1: *K2, p2* to end.
Rnd 2: As rnd 1.
Rnd 3: K.
Rnd 4: As rnd 3.
Rep rnds 1–4 for Texture St in the rnd until work
measures 4.5 (5, 6, 7.5) (9, 10, 11, 11.5)″ / 12 (13, 15, 19)
(23, 25, 28, 29) cm from CO edge or desired length to
start of armhole shaping and ending on rnd 2 of patt.

come out
and play!

DIVIDE FOR FRONT AND BACK

Beg working back and forth as foll, continuing Texture st flat:

Row 1: Ssk, k44 (48, 54, 58) (64, 70, 74, 80) sts, k2tog. Leave rem 48 (52, 58, 62) (68, 74, 78, 84) sts on waste yarn, turn.

Row 2: P.

Row 3: Ssk, patt as est to last 2 sts, k2tog.

Row 4: Patt as est.

Rep rows 3–4, 5 (5, 6, 6) (8, 9, 10, 11) more times. [34 (38, 42, 46) (48, 52, 54, 58) sts]

Cont in patt as est until armhole measures 2.5 (3, 3.25, 3.75) (4, 4.25, 4.5, 4.5)" / 6 (8, 8, 9) (10, 11, 11, 11) cm ending with a WS row.

SHAPE FRONT NECK

Row 1 (RS): Patt across next 10 (12, 13, 14) (15, 16, 16, 17) sts. Pl rem 24 (26, 29, 32) (33, 36, 38, 41) sts on waste yarn or st holder.

Working on these 10 (12, 13, 14) (15, 16, 16, 17) sts, work 13 (13, 15, 15) (17, 17, 19, 21) rows in patt as est, and at same time, dec 1 st at neck edge on next 0 (1, 0, 0) (0, 0, 0, 0) row, then every other row 2 (5, 3, 6) (4, 4, 2, 3) times, then every 3rd row 2 (0, 2, 0) (2, 2, 4, 4) times. [6 (6, 8, 8) (9, 10, 10, 10) sts]

Cont even in patt as est until the 13 (13, 15, 15) (17, 17, 19, 21) rows have been reached.

BO rem 6 (6, 8, 8) (9, 10, 10, 10) sts in patt as est.

With RS facing, join yarn to rem 24 (26, 29, 32) (33, 36, 38, 41) sts, BO next 14 (14, 16, 18) (18, 20, 22, 24) sts in patt for centre front neck, patt as est to end. [10 (12, 13, 14) (15, 16, 16, 17) sts]

Complete as for left side of neck.

BACK

Pl 48 (52, 58, 62) (68, 74, 78, 84) sts on waste yarn for back onto US 4 / 3.5 mm needles, ready to beg a RS row.

Row 1: Ssk, k44 (48, 54, 58) (64, 70, 74, 80) sts, k2tog.
Row 2: P.
Row 3: Ssk, patt as est to last 2 sts, k2tog.
Row 4: Patt as est.

Rep rows 3–4, 5 (5, 6, 6) (8, 9, 10, 11) more times. [34 (38, 42, 46) (48, 52, 54, 58) sts]

Cont in patt as est until armhole measures 1.5 (2, 2.25, 3.75) (4, 4.25, 4.5, 4.5)" / 4 (5, 6, 10) (10, 11, 12, 12) cm ending with a WS row.

Sizes 0–6 mos, 6–12 mos and 12–18 mos only
BACK OPENING

Row 1 (RS): Patt across next 17 (19, 21, –) (–, –, –, –) sts. Pl rem 17 (19, 21, –) (–, –, –, –) sts on waste yarn or st holder.

Cont in patt as est until armhole measures same length as front to start of neck shaping, but ending with a RS row.

SHAPE BACK NECK

Next Row (WS): BO 7 (7, 8, –) (–, –, –, –) sts in patt, patt to end. [10 (12, 13, –) (–, –, –, –) sts]

Working on these 10 (12, 13, –) (–, –, –, –) sts, work ** 12 (12, 14, –) (–, –, –, –) rows in patt as est, and at same time, dec 1 st at neck edge on next 0 (1, 0, –) (–, –, –, –) row, then every other row 2 (5, 3, –) (–, –, –, –) times, then every 3rd row 2 (0, 2, –) (–, –, –, –) time(s). [6 (6, 8, –) (–, –, –, –) sts]

BO rem 6 (6, 8, –) (–, –, –, –) sts in patt as est.

With RS facing, join yarn to rem 17 (19, 21, –) (–, –, –, –) sts and cont in patt as est until armhole measures same length as right back to start of neck shaping, but ending with a WS row.

Next Row (RS): BO 7 (7, 8, –) (–, –, –, –) sts in patt, patt to end. [10 (12, 13, –) (–, –, –, –) sts]

Complete as for right side, but working 13 (13, 15, –) (–, –, –, –) rows in texture pattern at **.

Sizes 2 yr, 4 yr, 6 yr, 8 yr and 10 yr only
SHAPE BACK NECK
Complete as for "Shape Front Neck".

All sizes resume
Join shoulders using 3-Needle Bind-Off.

NECKBAND

Note! Specific numbers for picking up the neckband and armbands are given. However, the exact number you end up with is not important, as long as you pick up the stitches evenly around and end with an even number of stitches.

With RS facing, US 2 / 2.75 mm set of DPNs or preferred needles for small circumference knitting and beg at centre back neck, pick up and k 68 (68, 76, 80) (88, 92, 100, 112) sts as foll:
7 (7, 8, 9) (9, 10, 11, 12) sts evenly across left back neck, 10 (10, 11, 11) (13, 13, 14, 16) sts evenly up slope of left back neck, 10 (10, 11, 11) (13, 13, 14, 16) sts evenly down slope of left front neck, 14 (14, 16, 18) (18, 20, 22, 24) sts evenly across front neck, 10 (10, 11, 11) (13, 13, 14, 16) sts evenly up slope of right front neck, 10 (10, 11, 11) (13, 13, 14, 16) sts evenly down slope of right back neck, 7 (7, 8, 9) (9, 10, 11, 12) sts evenly across right back neck.

Sizes 0–6 mos, 6–12 mos and 12–18 mos only
With WS facing and using Backwards Loop Method, CO 6 sts.
Row 1 (WS): *K1, p1* to end.
Row 2 (RS): As row 1.
Row 3: K1, p1, yo, k2tog (buttonhole made), p1, *k1, p1* to end.
Rows 4–5: As row 1
BO evenly in 1 x 1 rib patt.

Sizes 2 yr, 4 yr, 6 yr, 8 yr and 10 yr only
PM for BOR.
Rnd 1: *K1, p1* to end.
Rep last rnd 4 more times.
BO evenly in 1 x 1 rib patt.

ARMBANDS

With RS facing, US 2 / 2.75 mm set of DPNs or preferred needles for small circumference knitting and beg at bottom of armhole, pick up and k 33 (35, 40, 44) (48, 51, 56, 57) sts evenly up armhole edge to shoulder seam, pick up and k 33 (35, 40, 44) (48, 51, 56, 57) sts evenly down armhole edge to bottom of armhole.
PM for BOR. [66 (70, 80, 88) (96, 102, 112, 114) sts]

Rnd 1: *K1, p1* to end.
Rep last rnd 4 more times.
BO evenly in 1 x 1 rib patt.

Work second armband as first.

FINISHING

Weave in ends. Sizes 0–6 mos, 6–12 mos and 12–18 mos sew button to correspond to buttonhole on neckband. Block to measurements.

WHEAT

While many people are in awe of Canada's national parks and bustling cities, upon my arrival I was struck by the windswept prairie wheat fields. With this cardigan, I want to portray both the landscape — that golden, softly rustling expanse — and my childlike enthusiasm at encountering it for the first time.

SIZES

0–3 mos (3–6 mos, 6–12 mos, 12–18 mos, 2 yr) (4 yr, 6 yr, 8 yr, 10 yr)
Recommended ease: 2″ / 5 cm of positive ease at chest
Shown in size 4 yr on Ilana (height 38″ / 97 cm)

FINISHED MEASUREMENTS

Chest Circumference: 15.75 (17.75, 20, 22, 24.25) (26, 28.5, 30.25, 32.5)″ / 40 (44, 50, 55, 60) (65, 71, 76, 81) cm
Yoke Depth (front): 3.75 (4, 4.5, 5.5, 5.5) (6, 6, 6.25, 7)″ / 9.5 (10, 11.5, 14, 14) (15.25, 15.25, 16, 17.75) cm
Body Length to Underarm (front): 4 (4.5, 5, 5.5, 6) (7.5, 9, 10, 11)″ / 10 (11.5, 12.75, 14, 15.25) (19, 23, 25.5, 28) cm
Upper Arm Circumference: 6.75 (7.25, 8.5, 8.75, 9.5) (10.25, 11, 11.5, 11.75)″ / 17 (18, 21, 22, 24) (26, 28, 29, 30) cm
Sleeve Length to Underarm: 5.75 (6, 7, 8, 8.5) (10, 11.5, 13, 14)″ / 14 (15, 18, 20, 21) (25, 29, 33, 35) cm

MATERIALS

Yarn: 2 (2, 2, 2, 2) (3, 3, 4, 4) skeins of Tosh DK by Madeleinetosh (100% superwash merino wool, 225 yds / 205 m – 100 g), colourway Filtered Day Dreams
Or 231 (261, 330, 399, 447) (555, 641, 739, 838) yds / 212 (239, 302, 365, 409) (508, 587, 676, 767) m of DK-weight yarn

Needles: US 5 / 3.75 mm 16″ / 40 cm circular needles, 24″ / 60 cm and a set of DPNs. US 6 / 4 mm 16″ / 40 cm circular needles, 24″ / 60 cm and a set of DPNs

Notions: Stitch marker, waste yarn or stitch holders, tapestry needle, 5 (5, 5, 5, 6) (7, 7, 8, 9) small buttons

GAUGE

21 sts x 32 rows to 4″ / 10 cm on US 6 / 4 mm needles in St St, after blocking

SPECIAL ABBREVIATIONS

CDD: Central double decrease: Slip 2 sts together as if to knit to your RHN Knit the next stitch. Pass the slipped sts over the knit st. (2 sts dec'd)

NOTES

Sleeve instructions are written for DPNs. However, an alternate method of working small circumferences, such as Magic-Loop Method or short circular needles, can be used. As the yoke decreases, change to shorter circular needles when necessary.

The chart is read from bottom to top and from right to left on RS rows and from left to right on WS rows.

INSTRUCTIONS

The cardigan is worked from the bottom up. It features a circular yoke with a lacy garter ridge pattern. The sleeves are worked separately in the round to the base of the yoke. They are then joined to work the yoke. A section of short rows is worked at the bottom of the yoke for a more comfortable fit.

SLEEVES

Using US 5 / 3.75 mm set of DPNs, CO 30 (30, 34, 34, 36) (38, 38, 40, 40) sts using the Long-Tail CO Method, or your preferred method. Join in the rnd making sure sts are not twisted. PM for BOR.

Rnd 1: *K1, p1* to end.
Work in 1 x 1 rib as est until work measures 1″ / 2.5 cm from CO edge.

Change to US 6 / 4 mm DPNs or preferred needles for small circumference knitting.
K 7 (5, 5, 5, 5) (3, 5, 7, 7) rnds.

SLEEVE INCREASES
Inc Rnd: K1, m1l, k to 1 st bef BOR m, m1r, k1. (2 sts inc'd)
Rep inc rnd every 10th (8th, 8th, 8th, 7th) (8th, 7th, 8th, 8th) rnd 2 (3, 4, 5, 6) (7, 9, 9, 10) more times. [36 (38, 44, 46, 50) (54, 58, 60, 62) sts]

Work in St St in the rnd until sleeve measures 5.75 (6, 7, 8, 8.5) (10, 11.5, 13, 14)″ / 14 (15, 18, 20, 21) (25, 29, 33, 35) cm from CO edge, or desired length to underarm.
Next Rnd: K, ending 2 (2, 3, 3, 3) (3, 4, 4, 4) sts bef BOR m.

Pl next 3 (3, 5, 5, 5) (5, 7, 7, 7) sts on waste yarn or st holder for underarm, RM when come to it. Break yarn. [33 (35, 39, 41, 45) (49, 51, 53, 55) sts]

Set aside first sleeve, pl rem 33 (35, 39, 41, 45) (49, 51, 53, 55) sts on waste yarn or spare needle.

Work second sleeve as first.

BODY

BOTTOM HEM

Using US 5 / 3.75 mm 24" / 60 cm circular needles, CO 83 (93, 105, 115, 127) (137, 149, 159, 171) sts using the Long-Tail CO Method, or your preferred method. You will continue to work flat.

Row 1: *K1, p1* to last st, k1.
Row 2: P1, *k1, p1* to end.
Rep rows 1 and 2 until work measures 1" / 2.5 cm from CO edge, ending on a row 2 and inc 1 st at centre of last row, using an m1l. [84 (94, 106, 116, 128) (138, 150, 160, 172) sts]

Change to US 6 / 4 mm 24" / 60 cm circular needles. Work in St St until work measures 4 (4.5, 5, 5.5, 6) (7.5, 9, 10, 11)" / 10 (11.5, 13, 14, 15) (19, 23, 25, 28) cm from CO edge or desired length to underarm ending with RS facing for next row.

JOIN FOR YOKE

Next Row: K next 19 (21, 23, 26, 29) (31, 33, 36, 39) sts, pl next 3 (3, 5, 5, 5) (5, 7, 7, 7) sts onto waste yarn or st holder for right underarm. Transfer sts from one sleeve on to LHN of body, and k 33 (35, 39, 41, 45) (49, 51, 53, 55) sts for right sleeve. K across next 40 (46, 50, 54, 60) (66, 70, 74, 80) sts for back, pl next 3 (3, 5, 5, 5) (5, 7, 7, 7) sts onto waste yarn or st holder for left underarm. Transfer sts from rem sleeve on to LHN of body, and k 33 (35, 39, 41, 45) (49, 51, 53, 55) sts for left sleeve. K to end. [144 (158, 174, 188, 208) (226, 238, 252, 268) sts in total: 19 (21, 23, 26, 29) (31, 33, 36, 39) sts for each front, 33 (35, 39, 41, 45) (49, 51, 53, 55) sts for each sleeve and 40 (46, 50, 54, 60) (66, 70, 74, 80) sts for back]. 144, (158, 174, 188, 208) (226, 238, 252, 268) sts on needles.

WORK BACK YOKE SHORT ROWS

Short Row 1 (WS): P125 (137, 151, 162, 179) (195, 205, 216, 229), turn.
Short Row 2 (RS): MDS, k105 (115, 127, 135, 149) (163, 171, 179, 189), turn.
Short Row 3 (WS): MDS, p to 2 (2, 3, 3, 3) (5, 5, 5, 5) sts bef the DS, turn.
Short Row 4 (RS): MDS, k to 2 (2, 3, 3, 3) (5, 5, 5, 5) sts bef the DS, turn.
Rep short rows 3 and 4, 0 (0, 1, 1, 1) (2, 2, 2, 2) more time(s).

Next Short Row (WS): MDS, p to 3 (3, 5, 5, 5) (7, 7, 7, 7) sts bef the DS, turn.
Next Short Row (RS): MDS, k to 3 (3, 5, 5, 5) (7, 7, 7, 7) sts bef the DS, turn.
Next Row (WS): MDS, p to end of row, working the DSs as one (like a p2tog). [144 (158, 174, 188, 208) (226, 238, 252, 268) sts]
Adjustment Row (Dec): K6 (4, 8, 5, 1) (1, 12, 7, 11), *k2tog, k2 (2, 2, 3, 3) (3, 3, 3, 3), k2tog, k1 (2, 2, 2, 2) (2, 2, 3, 3)* to last 5 (2, 6, 3, 0) (0, 10, 5, 7) sts, k to end and at same time, working the rem DSs as one (like a k2tog). [106 (120, 134, 148, 162) (176, 190, 204, 218) sts]

Work 1 (3, 5, 1, 1) (3, 3, 7, 1) row(s) in St St. RS is facing for next row.

YOKE

Beg to work yoke as foll:
Set-Up Row: Reading RS rows from right to left and WS rows from left to right, beg working from Chart as foll: Work row 25 (25, 25, 13, 13) (3, 13, 13, 1) of chart, working 14-st rep 7 (8, 9, 10, 11) (12, 13, 14, 15) times to last 8 sts, work last 8 sts as indicated on chart.
Next Row: Work first 8 sts as indicated on Row 26 (26, 26, 14, 14) (14, 14, 14, 2) of chart, work 14-st rep 7 (8, 9, 10, 11) (12, 13, 14, 15) times to end of row.
Cont as est until the 48th row of chart has been completed. [78 (88, 98, 108, 118) (128, 138, 148, 158) sts]

Adjustment Row (Dec): K3 (2, 1, 3, 2) (1, 3, 2, 1), *k2tog, k1* to last 3 (2, 1, 3, 2) (1, 3, 2, 1) sts, k to end. [54 (60, 66, 74, 80) (86, 94, 100, 106) sts]

P 1 row.

Leave these sts on the needle.

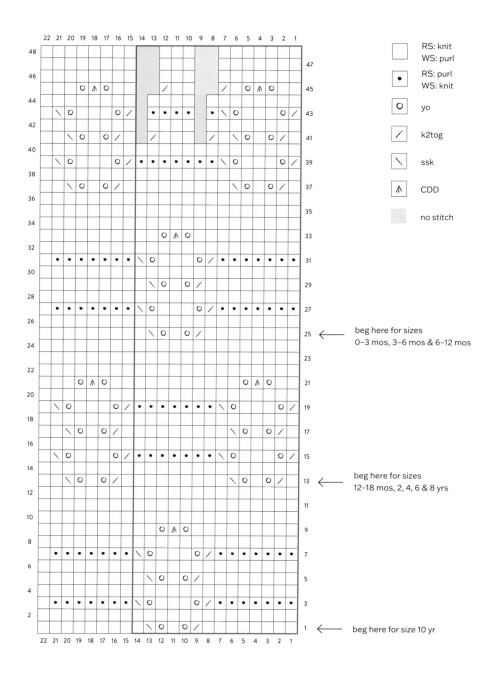

RS: knit
WS: purl

RS: purl
WS: knit

○ yo

／ k2tog

＼ ssk

⋀ CDD

no stitch

beg here for sizes
0–3 mos, 3–6 mos & 6–12 mos

beg here for sizes
12–18 mos, 2, 4, 6 & 8 yrs

beg here for size 10 yr

BUTTON BANDS

LEFT FRONT BUTTON BAND

With RS facing and using US 5 / 3.75 mm 24" / 60 cm circular needles, pick up and k 42 (48, 54, 58, 60) (72, 82, 92, 100) sts (approx. 3 sts for every 4 rows) evenly down left front edge.

Row 1: *K1, p1* to end.
Rep row 1, 4 more times.
BO evenly in 1 x 1 rib patt.

RIGHT FRONT BUTTONHOLE BAND

With RS facing and using US 5 / 3.75 mm 24" / 60 cm circular needles, pick up and k sts as bef, evenly up right front edge and ending with same number of sts as for button band.

Row 1: *K1, p1* to end.
Rep row 1 once more.

Next Row (make buttonholes): K1, p1, *k2tog, yo, (k1, p1) 3 (4, 5, 5, 4) (5, 5, 5, 5) times*, rep from *–* 3 (3, 3, 3, 4) (5, 5, 6, 7) more times, k2tog, yo, *k1, p1* 3 (2, 1, 3, 3) (1, 3, 2, 1) times.
Rep row 1, 2 more times.
BO evenly in 1 x 1 rib.

NECKBAND

Using US 5 / 3.75 mm 24" / 60 cm circular needles, and starting at top of Right Front Buttonhole Band, pick up and k 4 sts across top of band, *k1, p1*, rep *–* across 54 (60, 66, 74, 80) (86, 94, 100, 106) sts from top of yoke, pick up and k 4 sts across top of Left Front Button Band. [62 (68, 74, 82, 88) (94, 102, 108, 114) sts]

Row 1: *K1, p1* to end.
Rep row 1, 4 more times.
BO evenly in 1 x 1 rib.

FINISHING

Use 3-Needle Bind-Off or Grafting to join underarm sts. Weave in ends, closing any gaps that rem at the underarms. Sew buttons to correspond to buttonholes on left front button band. Block to measurements.

WRITTEN INSTRUCTIONS FOR CHART
(Worked over a multiple of 14 + 8 sts)

Size 10 yr starts here
Row 1 (RS): *K8, k2tog, yo, k1, yo, ssk, k1* to last 8 sts, k8.
Row 2 and all even rnds: P.
Row 3: *P7, k2tog, yo, k3, yo, ssk* to last 8 sts, p7, k1.
Row 5: As row 1.
Row 7: As row 3.
Row 9: *K9, yo, CDD, yo, k2* to last 8 sts, k8.
Row 11: K.
Row 12: P.

Sizes 12–18 mos, 2 yr, 4 yr, 6 yr and 8 yr start here
Row 13 (RS): *K1, k2tog, yo, k1, yo, ssk, k8* to last 8 sts, k1, k2tog, yo, k1, yo, ssk, k2.
Row 15: *K2tog, yo, k3, yo, ssk, p7* to last 8 sts, k2tog, yo, k3, yo, ssk, k1.
Row 17: As row 13.
Row 19: As row 15.
Row 21: *K2, yo, CDD, yo, k9* to last 8 sts, k2, yo, CDD, yo, k3.
Row 23: K.
Row 24: P.

Sizes 0–3 mos and 3–6 mos start here
Row 25 (RS): *K8, k2tog, yo, k1, yo, ssk, k1* to last 8 sts, k8.
Row 27: *P7, k2tog, yo, k3, yo, ssk* to last 8 sts, p7, k1.
Row 29: As row 25.
Row 31: As row 27.
Row 33: *K9, yo, CDD, yo, k2* to last 8 sts, k8.
Row 35: K.
Row 37: *K1, k2tog, yo, k1, yo, ssk, k8* to last 8 sts, k1, k2tog, yo, k1, yo, ssk, k2.
Row 39: *K2tog, yo, k3, yo, ssk, p7* to last 8 sts, k2tog, yo, k3, yo, ssk, k1.
Row 41: *K1, k2tog, yo, k1, yo, ssk, k1, k2tog, k3, k2tog* to last 8 sts, k1, k2tog, yo, k1, yo, ssk, k2. (2 sts per rep dec'd)
Row 43: *K2tog, yo, k3, yo, ssk, p5* to last 8 sts, k2tog, yo, k3, yo, ssk, k1.
Row 45: *K2, yo, CDD, yo, k1, k2tog, k2, k2tog* to last 8 sts, k2, yo, CDD, yo, k3. (2 sts per rep dec'd)
Row 47: K.
Row 48: P.

DEAR DEER

I designed this blanket in honour of my daughter, my little deer, as I lovingly refer to her. It is simple enough to fit into any interior but also whimsical enough to capture the attention of your tiny one.

SIZE

One Size

FINISHED MEASUREMENTS

Length: 40" / 102 cm
Width: 33" / 84 cm

MATERIALS

Yarn: Heavy Merino by Knitting for Olive (100% merino wool, 137 yards / 125 m – 50 g)
5 skeins of colourway Oatmeal (MC)
1 skein of each colourway Brown Nougat (A), Marzipan (B), Copper (C), Mouse Gray (D) and Dusty Petroleum Blue (E)
Or approx. the foll amounts of worsted-weight yarn:
685 yds / 625 m of MC
137 yds / 125 m each of A, B, C, D and E

Needles: US 7 / 4.5 mm 32" / 80 circular needles, or longer if desired

Notions: Tapestry needle

GAUGE

20 sts x 26 rows to 4" / 10 cm on US 7 / 4.5 mm needles in St St, after blocking.

19.5 sts x 25 rows to 4" / 10 cm on US 7 / 4.5 mm needles in Broken Double Seed St Patt, after blocking.

NOTES

The border panels are worked using charts.

The charts are read from bottom to top and from right to left on RS rows and from left to right on WS rows. When working stranded colourwork, keep floats in the back loose to maintain stretch. For floats longer than 5 stitches, twist yarns together in the back.

INSTRUCTIONS

The blanket is worked flat. It is made up of 3 main panels: two border panels worked in stranded colourwork and a centre panel worked in a broken double seed stitch pattern.

CAST-ON

With MC, CO 142 sts using the Long-Tail CO Method, or your preferred method. You will cont to work flat.

BORDER PANEL

Row 1 (RS): P.
Row 2 (WS): K.
Row 3: K1, *k2, p2* to last st, k1.
Row 4: P1, *k2, p2* to last st, p1.
Row 5: K1, *p2, k2* to last st, k1.
Row 6: P1, *p2, k2* to last st, p1.
Rows 7–8: As rows 3–4.
Next Row (RS): P.
Next Row (WS): K, m1l at centre of row. [143 sts]
Next Row: *With A, k1, with MC, k1* to last st, with A, k1. Break MC.
Next Row: With A, p.
Next Row: *With A, k1, with B, k1* to last st, with A, k1. Break A.
Next Row: With B, p.

With RS facing, beg working from Chart A as foll:
Beg where indicated on the chart, work first 2 sts, work the 9-st rep 15 times to last 6 sts, work last 6 sts as indicated on the chart.
Cont in this manner as est until 8 rows of Chart A have been completed.

Next Row: *With A, k1, with B, k1* to last st, with A, k1. Break B.
Next Row: With A, p.
Next Row: *With A, k1, with D, k1* to last st, with A, k1. Break A.
Next Row: With D, p.

Beg working from Chart B: Beg where indicated on the chart, work the 47-st rep 3 times to last 2 sts, work last 2 sts as indicated on the chart. Cont in this manner as est until 16 rows of Chart B have been completed.

Next Row: *With A, k1, with D, k1* to last st, with A, k1. Break D.
Next Row: With A, p.
Next Row: *With A, k1, with B, k1* to last st, with A, k1. Break A.
Next Row: With B, p.

Work from Chart C in same manner as Chart A until 8 rows of Chart C have been completed.

Next Row: *With A, k1, with B, k1* to last st, with A, k1. Break B.
Next Row: With A, p.
Next Row: *With A, k1, with MC, k1* to last st, with A, k1. Break A.
Next Row: With MC, p.

CENTRE PANEL

Next Row: K, inc 1 st at centre of row, using an m1l. [144 sts]
Next Row: P.
Work 2 more rows St St.

Beg Broken Double Seed St Patt as foll:
Row 1: K1, p2, *k2, p2* to last st, k1.
Row 2: P3, *k2, p2* to last st, p1.
Row 3: K.
Row 4: P.
Rows 5–6: As rows 3–4.
Row 7: As row 3.
Row 8: As row 2.
Row 9: As row 1.
Row 10: As row 4.
Rows 11–14: As rows 3–6.
Rep rows 1–14, 7 more times.
Rep rows 1–13 once more.
Next Row: P, dec 1 st at centre of row, using a p2tog. [143 sts]

BORDER PANEL

Next Row: *With A, k1, with MC, k1* to last st, with A, k1. Break MC.
Next Row: With A, p.
Next Row: *With A, k1, with B, k1* to last st, with A, k1. Break A.
Next Row: With B, p.

Work from Chart C in same manner until 8 rows of Chart C have been completed.

Next Row: *With A, k1, with B, k1* to last st, with A, k1. Break B.
Next Row: With A, p.
Next Row: *With A, k1, with D, k1* to last st, with A, k1. Break A.
Next Row: With D, p.

Work from Chart D in same manner until 16 rows of Chart D have been completed.

Next Row: *With A, k1, with D, k1* to last st, with A, k1. Break D.
Next Row: With A, p.
Next Row: *With A, k1, with B, k1* to last st, with A, k1. Break A.
Next Row: With B, p.

Work from Chart A in same manner until 8 rows of Chart A have been completed.

Next Row: *With A, k1, with B, k1* to last st, with A, k1. Break B.
Next Row: With A, p.
Next Row: *With A, k1, with MC, k1* to last st, with A, k1. Break A.
Next Row (WS): With MC, k.
Next Row (RS): P, dec 1 st at centre of row, using a p2tog. [142 sts]
Row 1 (WS): P1, *k2, p2* to last st, p1.
Row 2 (RS): K1, *k2, p2* to last st, k1.
Row 3: P1, *p2, k2* to last st, p1.
Row 4: K1, *p2, k2* to last st, k1.
Rows 5–6: As rows 1–2.
Next Row (WS): K.
BO evenly pwise.

EDGING

With RS facing and A, pick up and k approx. 3 sts for every 4 rows evenly along one long edge of blanket. K 3 rows. BO evenly kwise. Rep along the rem long edge.

FINISHING

Weave in ends. Block to measurements.

CHART A

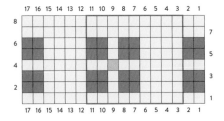

CHART C

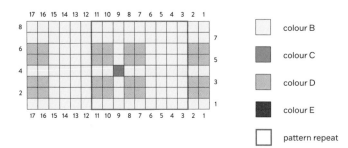

	colour B
	colour C
	colour D
	colour E
	pattern repeat

CHART B

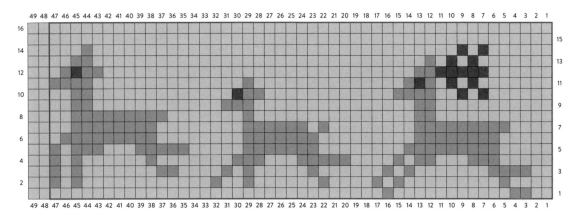

CHART D

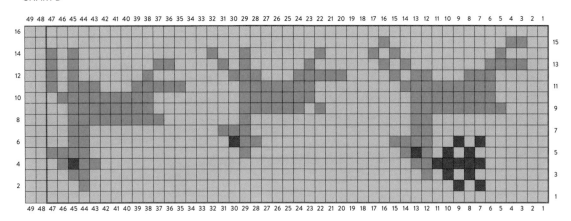

PISCUCHA TEE

As a child in El Salvador, I used to make kites with my friends. We cut out large pieces of cardboard and glued beautiful bits of paper onto them. Piscucha Tee reminds me of those windy days full of laughter. Wear it on its own, or with a long-sleeved shirt underneath — it is perfect for any weather!

SIZES

0–3 mos (3–6 mos, 6–12 mos, 12–18 mos, 2 yr) (4 yr, 6 yr, 8 yr, 10 yr)
Recommended ease: 2" / 5 cm positive ease

FINISHED MEASUREMENTS

Chest Circumference: 17 (19, 21, 23, 25) (27, 29, 31, 33)" / 43 (48, 53, 58, 63) (68, 73, 78, 83) cm
Yoke Depth (front): 4.25 (4.25, 5, 5.5, 5.5) (6, 6.5, 7, 7.5)" / 11 (11, 13, 14, 14) (14, 17, 18, 19) cm
Body Length to Underarm (front): 3 (3.5, 4, 4.5, 5.5) (6, 6.5, 7, 7.5)" / 8 (9, 10, 11, 14) (15, 16, 18, 19) cm
Upper Arm Circumference: 6 (6, 7, 7, 7) (9, 9, 10, 11)" / 15 (15, 18, 18, 18) (23, 23, 25, 28) cm
Sleeve Length to Underarm: 1.25 (1.25, 1.25, 1.5, 1.5) (1.5, 2, 2, 2)" / 3 (3, 3, 3, 3) (3, 5, 5, 5) cm

MATERIALS

Yarn:
Pink version shown in size 4 yr on Amanda (38" / 97 cm)
Cashmere Classic by Cardiff (100% Italian spun cashmere, 120 yds / 109 m – 25 g) as folls:
Main Colour MC: 2 (2, 2, 2, 3) (3, 4, 5, 5) balls, colourway Loop 718
1 ball each of Contrast Colour A, colourway Panna 599, Contrast Colour B, colourway Bloom 597 and Contrast Colour C, colourway Zen 687

Brown version shown in size 4 yr on Ilana (38" / 97 cm)
Chickadee Organic Heathers by Quince & Co. (100% organic wool, 164 yds / 150 m – 50 g) as folls:
Main Colour MC: 1 (2, 2, 2, 3) (3, 3, 4, 4) balls, colourway Cedar 162
1 ball each of Contrast Colour A, colourway Caspian 155, Contrast Colour B, colourway Jasper 161 and Contrast Colour C, colourway Audouin 157

Or sport-weight yarn as folls:
Main Colour MC: 150 (190, 230, 280, 350) (425, 500, 570, 640) yds / 140 (175, 210, 260, 320) (340, 460, 525, 590) m
Contrast Colour A: 30 (35, 40, 50, 55) (65, 75, 90, 100) yds / 27 (32, 36, 45, 50) (60, 70, 82, 92) m
Contrast Colour B: 18 (22, 28, 32, 35) (40, 50, 58, 64) yds / 16 (20, 25, 29, 32) (36, 45, 53, 58) m

Contrast Colour C: 5 (6, 7, 7, 7) (10, 10, 12, 14) yds / 5 (5, 7, 7, 7) (10, 10, 11, 13) m

Needles: US 4 / 3.5 mm 16" / 40 cm (optional for child sizes), 24" / 60 cm circular needles and a set of DPNs

Notions: Stitch markers (3 total, 1 unique for BOR), stitch holders or waste yarn, tapestry needle, 1 button for sizes 0–3 mos to 2 yr only

GAUGE

28 sts x 34 rnds to 4" / 10 cm on US 4 / 3.5 mm needles in St St, after blocking

28 sts x 32 rnds to 4" / 10 cm on US 4 / 3.5 mm needles over colourwork, after blocking

NOTES

Neck and sleeve instructions are written for DPNs. However, an alternate method of working small circumferences, such as Magic-Loop Method or short circular needles, can be used. As the yoke increases, change to a longer circular needle when necessary.

The yoke is worked from charts. Charts are read from bottom to top and from right to left when knitting in the rnd. When working stranded colourwork, keep floats in the back loose to maintain stretch. For floats longer than 5 sts, twist yarns together in the back.

INSTRUCTIONS

The tee is knit from the top down with circular yoke. A section of short rows is worked at the bottom of the yoke to create the small capped sleeves. The bottom hem has optional side split openings.

NECK EDGE
Sizes 0–3 mos, 3–6 mos, 6–12 mos, 12–18 mos and 2 yr only
With US 4 / 3.5 mm 16" / 40 cm circular needles and A, CO 72 (75, 75, 78, 84) (–, –, –, –) sts using the Long-Tail CO Method, or your preferred method. Do not join in the rnd.
Working back and forth on the circular needles, p 1 row.

Next Row: K2, yo, k2tog (buttonhole made), k to end.
Next Row: P.
Next Row (WS): BO 6 sts pwise for button tab, p to end, turn. RS is facing. Join in rnd. Pl BOR m (centre back neck). [66 (69, 69, 72, 78) (–, –, –, –) sts]

Sizes 4 yr, 6 yr, 8 yr and 10 yr only
With US 4 / 3.5 mm set of DPNs or 16" / 40 cm circular needles and A, CO – (–, –, –, –) (81, 84, 90, 93) sts using the Long-Tail CO Method, or your preferred method. Join in the rnd making sure sts are not twisted. PM for BOR (centre back neck).
Rnd 1: P.
Rep rnd 1 twice more.

Sizes 0–3 mos, 3–6 mos and 2 yr only
Next Rnd (Inc): With B, k8 (9, –, –, 5) (–, –, –, –), *m1l, k3* to last 4 (6, –, –, 1) (–, –, –, –) sts, k to BOR. [84 (87, –, –, 102) (–, –, –, –) sts]

Sizes 6–12 mos, 6 yr and 10 yr only
Next Rnd (Inc): With B, k– (–, 2, –, –) (–, 1, –, 1), *m1l, k– (–, 2, –, –) (–, 1, –, 1)* – (–, 3, –, –) (–, 2, –, 2) times, *m1l, k3* to last – (–, 7, –, –) (–, 3, –, 3) sts, *m1l, k– (–, 2, –, –) (–, 1, –, 1)* – (–, 3, –, –) (–, 2, –, 2) times, k1. [– (–, 93, –, –) (–, 114, –, 126) sts]

Sizes 12–18 mos, 4 yr and 8 yr only
Next Rnd (Inc): With B, *k3, m1l* to end. [– (–, –, 96, –) (108, –, 120, –) sts]

BEGIN YOKE PATTERN
Change to longer circular needle when necessary. Beg working yoke patt from Chart A, rep 28 (29, 31, 32, 34) (36, 38, 40, 42) times around until 9 rnds of chart are complete. [140 (145, 155, 160, 170) (180, 190, 200, 210) sts]

Size 0–3 mos only
Next Rnd (Inc): With A, *k7, m1l* to end. (160 sts)

Size 3–6 mos only
Next Rnd (Inc): With A, k1, m1l, k2, *m1l, k5* to last 2 sts, m1l, k2. (175 sts)

Size 6–12 mos only
Next Rnd (Inc): With A, k10, *m1l, k 4* to last 5 sts, k to end. (190 sts)

Size 12–18 mos only
Next Rnd (Inc): With A, k1, m1l, k4, *m1l, k3, m1l, k4* to last st, k1. (205 sts)

Size 2 yr only
Next Rnd (Inc): With A, k1, *m1l, k2* 3 times, *m1l, k4* to last 7 sts, *m1l, k2* 3 times, k1. (215 sts)

Size 4 yr only
Next Rnd (Inc): With A, *k3, m1l* to end. (240 sts)

Size 6 yr only
Next Rnd (Inc): With A, k9, *m1l, k2, m1l, k3* to last 6 sts, k to end. (260 sts)

Size 8 yr only
Next Rnd (Inc): With A, k8, m1l, k3, *m1l, k2, m1l, k3* to last 4 sts, k to end. (275 sts)

Size 10 yr only
Next Rnd (Inc): With A, k1, m1l, k1, *m1l, k2, m1l, k3* to last 3 sts, *m1l, k1* 2 times, k1. (295 sts)

All sizes resume
Beg working from Chart B, rep 32 (35, 38, 41, 43) (48, 52, 55, 59) times around until 11 (11, 18, 18, 18) (18, 18, 18, 18) rnds of chart are complete. [192 (210, 228, 246, 258) (288, 312, 330, 354) sts]

Adjustment Rnd: With A, k, inc 3 (0, 2, 4, 2) (2, 3, 0, 1) st(s) evenly around, using an m1l. [195 (210, 230, 250, 260) (290, 315, 330, 355) sts]

With A, k 0 (0, 0, 1, 1) (1, 1, 1, 1) rnd.

Beg working from Chart C, working the 5-st rep 39 (42, 46, 50, 52) (58, 63, 66, 71) times around until 6 rnds of chart are complete.

With MC, k 0 (1, 0, 2, 2) (6, 10, 14, 18) rnd(s).

WORK BACK YOKE SHORT ROWS
Short Row 1 (RS): With A, k56 (60, 68, 76, 78) (87, 93, 106, 112), turn.
Short Row 2 (WS): MDS, p to BOR, SM, p56 (60, 68, 76, 78) (87, 93, 106, 112), turn.
Short Row 3 (RS): MDS, k to BOR, SM, k to 2 (2, 2, 3, 3) (3, 3, 3, 3) sts bef the DS, turn.

Short Row 4 (WS): MDS, p to BOR, SM, p to 2 (2, 2, 3, 3) (3, 3, 3, 3) sts bef the DS, turn.

Sizes 0–3 mos and 3–6 mos only
Short Row 5 (RS): MDS, k to BOR, SM, k to 3 sts bef the DS, turn.
Short Row 6 (WS): MDS, p to BOR, SM, p to 3 sts bef the DS, turn.

Sizes 6–12 mos, 12–18 mos, 2 yr, 4 yr, 6 yr, 8 yr and 10 yr only
Short Row 5 (RS): MDS, k to BOR, SM, k to – (–, 2, 3, 3) (3, 3, 4, 4) sts bef the DS, turn.
Short Row 6 (WS): MDS, p to BOR, SM, p to – (–, 2, 3, 3) (3, 3, 4, 4) sts bef the DS, turn.
Short Row 7 (RS): MDS, k to BOR, SM, k to – (–, 3, 4, 4) (4, 4, 5, 5) sts bef the DS, turn.
Short Row 8 (WS): MDS, p to BOR, SM, p to – (–, 3, 4, 4) (4, 4, 5, 5) sts bef the DS, turn.
Rep short rows 7 and 8, – (–, 0, 0, 0) (0, 0, 1, 1) more time.

All sizes resume
Next Rnd (RS): MDS, k back to BOR, SM, then k 1 rnd working each DS as one st (like a k2tog). [195 (210, 230, 250, 260) (290, 315, 330, 355) sts]

DIVIDE FOR BODY
Next Rnd: Leave BOR in pl, k27 (31, 34, 38, 38) (41, 45, 47, 51), pl next 41 (42, 45, 47, 49) (57, 63, 64, 70) sts for sleeve onto waste yarn or holder, using Backwards Loop Method, CO 5 (5, 5, 5, 9) (9, 9, 10, 10) sts for underarm, PM for side, k59 (64, 72, 80, 86) (94, 99, 108, 113), pl next 41 (42, 45, 47, 49) (57, 63, 64, 70) sts for sleeve onto waste yarn or holder, PM for side, using Backwards Loop Method, CO 5 (5, 5, 5, 9) (9, 9, 10, 10) sts for underarm, k to end of rnd. [123 (136, 150, 166, 180) (194, 207, 222, 235) body sts]

Size 0–3 mos only
Adjustment Rnd: K to first side m, SM, k2tog, k to next m, SM, k to end. 122 sts There are 58 sts in front and 64 sts in back.

Sizes 3–6 mos, 6–12 mos, 12–18 mos, 2 yr, 4 yr and 8 yr only
Next Rnd: K to first side m, SM, k to next m, SM, k to end. [– (136, 150, 166, 180, 194, –, 222, –) sts] [There are – (64, 72, 80, 86) (94, –, 108, –) sts in front and – (72, 78, 86, 94) (100, –, 114, –) sts in back.]

Sizes 6 yr and 10 yr only
Adjustment Rnd: K to first side m, SM, k1, m1l, k to next m, SM, k to end. [– (–, –, –, –) (–, 208, –, 236) sts] [There are – (–, –, –, –) (–, 100, –, 114) sts in front and – (–, –, –, –) (–, 108, –, 122) sts in back.]

All sizes resume
Work in St St until body measures 2 (2.5, 3, 3.5, 4.5) (5, 5.5, 6, 6.5)" / 5 (6, 9, 10, 11) (12, 13, 15, 16) cm from underarm or 1" / 2.5 cm less than desired length to start of bottom hem.

BOTTOM HEM WITH SIDE SPLIT OPENINGS

BOTTOM BACK HEM
Beg working back and forth in rows as folls:
Row 1 (RS): K to first side m, turn. RM.
Row 2 (WS): P2, *k1, p1* to BOR m, RM, k1, p2tog, *k1, p1* to 3 sts bef next side m, k1, p2, turn. RM. [63 (71, 77, 85, 93) (99, 107, 113, 121) sts]
Row 3: K2, p1, *k1, p1* to last 2 sts, k2.
Row 4: P2, *k1, p1* to last st, p1.
Rep rows 3 and 4 twice more.
BO evenly in rib patt as est.

BOTTOM FRONT HEM
With WS facing and beg at side seam, join MC to rem 58 (64, 72, 80, 86) (94, 100, 108, 114) sts. Beg working back and forth in rows as folls:
Row 1 (WS): P2, *k1, p1* over next 26 (28, 32, 36, 40) (44, 46, 50, 54) sts, k1, p2tog, *k1, p1* to last st, p1. [57 (63, 71, 79, 85) (93, 99, 107, 113) sts]
Row 2: K2, p1, *k1, p1* to last 2 sts, k2.
Row 3: P2, *k1, p1* to last st, p1.
Rep rows 2 and 3 twice more.
BO evenly in rib patt as est.

BOTTOM HEM VERSION NO SIDE SPLITS

Rnd 1: *K1, p1* to end.
Cont in est 1 x 1 rib for 6 more rnds.
BO evenly in 1 x 1 rib patt.

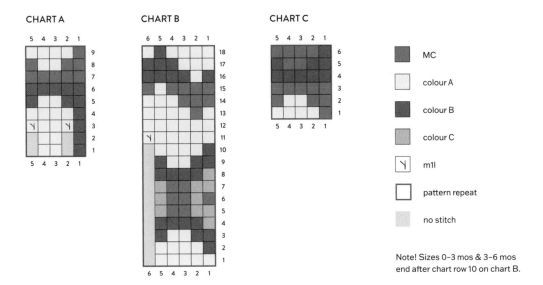

CHART A

CHART B

CHART C

■	MC
□	colour A
■	colour B
▨	colour C
Ɲ	m1l
☐	pattern repeat
▨	no stitch

Note! Sizes 0–3 mos & 3–6 mos end after chart row 10 on chart B.

SLEEVES

Pl 41 (42, 45, 47, 49) (57, 63, 64, 70) sts on waste yarn for sleeve onto US 4 / 3.5 mm set of DPNs or preferred style for working small circumferences. Beg at centre of underarm, join MC and pick up and k2 (2, 3, 3, 3) (3, 3, 4, 4) sts along underarm CO sts, k41 (42, 45, 47, 49) (57, 63, 64, 70) sts from sleeve, and then pick up and k1 (2, 2, 2, 3) (3, 3, 3, 3) sts along underarm CO to centre. PM for BOR. [44 (46, 50, 52, 55) (63, 69, 71, 77) sts]

Sizes 2 yr, 4 yr, 6 yr, 8 yr and 10 yr only
Adjustment Rnd: K to last 3 sts, k2tog, k1. [– (–, –, –, 54) (62, 68, 70, 76) sts]

All sizes resume
Dec Rnd: K1, ssk, k to 3 sts from end, k2tog, k1. (2 sts dec'd)
K 1 rnd.
Work dec rnd 0 (0, 0, 0, 0) (0, 1, 1, 1) more time. [42 (44, 48, 50, 52) (60, 64, 66, 72) sts]
K 0 (0, 0, 1, 0) (0, 0, 3, 3) rnd(s).

Adjustment Rnd: K5 (6, 5, 6, 19) (11, 8, 9, 10), *k2tog, k4 (4, 3, 5, 10) (10, 7, 7, 5)* to last 1 (2, 3, 2, 9) (1, 2, 3, 6) st(s), k to end. [36 (38, 40, 44, 50) (56, 58, 60, 64) sts]
Cuff Rnd 1: *K1, p1* to end.
Cont in est 1 x 1 rib for 4 more rnds.
BO evenly in 1 x 1 rib patt.

Work second sleeve as first.

FINISHING

Weave in ends, closing any gaps that rem at the underarms. Sizes up to 2 yrs sew button to correspond to buttonhole on neckband. Block to measurements.

These mitts make a great pair with the Piscucha Tee.
However, they look good as a stand-out piece with
another kind of outfit too!

PISCUCHA
MITTS

SIZES

2–6 yrs (8–10 yrs)

FINISHED MEASUREMENTS

Circumference: 5 (5.75)" / 13 (14) cm
Length: 8" / 20.5 cm

MATERIALS

YARN:
Pink version
Cashmere Classic by Cardiff (100% Italian spun
cashmere, 120 yds / 109 m – 25 g) as folls:
1 (2) ball(s) Main Colour MC, colourway Loop 718
1 (1) ball Contrast Colour A, colourway Zen 687
1 (1) ball Contrast Colour B, colourway Bloom 597

Light brown version
Fingering by Tukuwool (100% Finnish wool, 219 yds /
200 m – 50 g) as folls:
1 (1) skein Main Colour MC, colourway Hiesu 37
1 (1) skein Contrast Colour A, colourway Yrtti 36
1 (1) skein Contrast Colour B, colourway Rohto H36

Or 120 (138) yds / 109 (126) m each of MC, A and B of
sport-weight yarn

Needles: US 4 / 3.5 mm set of DPNs

Notions: Stitch markers, stitch holders or waste yarn,
tapestry needle

GAUGE

28 sts x 34 rnds to 4" / 10 cm on US 4 / 3.5 mm needles
in St St, after blocking

28 sts x 32 rnds to 4" / 10 cm on US 4 / 3.5 mm needles
over colour stranding, after blocking

NOTES

This pattern is written for DPNs. However, an alternate
method of working small circumferences, such as
Magic Loop Method, can be used.

Charts are read from bottom to top and from right to
left when knitting in the rnd.

INSTRUCTIONS

The mitts are worked in the round starting with the cuff.
The thumb is completed by a Backwards Loop Cast-On.
Charts are used to work the body of the mitt.

RIGHT MITT

*With US 4 / 3.5 mm set of DPNs and yarn A, CO 34 (38)
sts using the Long-Tail CO Method, or your preferred
method. Evenly disperse sts over 4 DPNs. Join in the
rnd making sure sts are not twisted. PM for BOR.
Rnd 1: *K1, p1* to end.
Cont in est 1 x 1 rib for 5 more rnds or to desired length
for cuff.

Next Rnd: K, inc 2 (4) sts evenly around, using an m1l.
[36 (42) sts]
K 5 rnds.

Beg working from Chart A, working the 6-st rep 6
(7) times around until the 6th rnd of chart has been
completed, and joining yarns A and B as needed.

With A, k 1 rnd.
Next Rnd (Adjustment): With A, k dec 1 (2) sts evenly
around. [35 (40) sts]

Beg working from Chart B, working the 5-st rep 7 (8)
times around until 6 rnds of chart have been completed.
With A, k 1 rnd.
Next Rnd (Adjustment): With A, k inc 1 (2) sts evenly
around, using an m1l. – [36 (42) sts]

Beg working from Chart A, working the 6-st rep 6 (7)
times around until 11 rnds of chart have been completed.
With MC, k 3 rnds.
Next Rnd (Adjustment): With MC, k dec 1 (2) sts evenly
around. [35 (40) sts]

Beg working from Chart C, working the 5-st rep 7 (8)
times around until 6 rnds of chart have been completed.
With MC, k 3 rnds.*

CHART A	CHART B	CHART C	CHART D

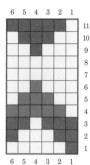 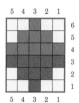 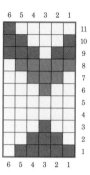

- MC
- colour A
- colour B
- pattern repeat

DIVIDE FOR THUMB

Next Rnd: With MC, k3 (5), sl next 8 (9) sts onto st holder or waste yarn for thumb, using Backwards Loop Method, CO 8 (9) sts, k to end, inc 1 (2) sts evenly around, using an m1l. [36 (42) sts]

**Beg working from Chart D, working the 6-st rep 6 (7) times around until 11 rnds of chart have been completed.

With A, k 1 rnd.
Next Rnd: *K1, p1* to end.
Cont in est 1 x 1 rib 4 more times.
BO evenly in 1 x 1 rib.

THUMB

Pl 8 (9) sts from st holder or waste yarn onto US 4 / 3.5 mm set of DPNs and beg at CO edge, join MC and pick up and k 10 (11) sts along the CO sts, filling in the gaps, k8 (9) from thumb. PM for BOR. [18 (20) sts]
K 3 rnds.

Next Rnd: *K1, p1* to end.
Cont in est 1 x 1 rib 5 more times.
BO evenly in 1 x 1 rib.**

LEFT MITT

Work as for Right Mitt *–*.

DIVIDE FOR THUMB

Next Rnd: With MC, k24 (26), inc 1 (2) sts evenly across, using an m1l, sl next 8 (9) sts onto st holder or waste yarn for thumb, using the Backwards Loop Method, CO 8 (9) sts, k to end. [36 (42) sts]

Complete as for Right Mitt from **–**.

FINISHING

Weave in all ends. Block to measurements if desired.

LUCA

This cardigan takes my mind to chilly summer nights at the cottage. It is a wardrobe staple that goes with everything: overalls, dresses, jeans — or whatever fashion your little one is currently into!

SIZES

0–3 mos (3–6 mos, 6–12 mos, 12–18 mos, 2 yr) (4 yr, 6 yr, 8 yr, 10 yr)
Recommended ease: 2" / 5 cm of positive ease

FINISHED MEASUREMENTS

Chest Circumference: 15.25 (17.5, 19, 21, 23.25) (25.5, 27, 29, 31.25)" / 48 (44, 47, 53, 58) (64, 67, 73, 78) cm
Body Length to Underarm (front): 4 (4.5, 5, 5.5, 6) (7, 8, 8.5, 9)" / 10 (12, 13, 14, 15) (18, 21, 22, 23) cm
Raglan Depth: 3.25 (3.5, 4, 4.25, 4.25) (5.25, 5.5, 6, 6.25)" / 8 (8, 10, 11, 11) (13, 14, 15, 16) cm
Upper Arm Circumference: 6.5 (7, 7.75, 8.25, 9) (10.25, 10.5, 11.25, 11.75)" / 16.5 (18, 19, 21, 23) (25, 26, 28, 29) cm
Sleeve Length to Underarm: 5.75 (6, 7, 8, 8.5) (9.75, 11.5, 13, 14)" / 15 (15, 18, 20, 21) (25, 28, 32, 35) cm

MATERIALS

Yarn:
Cream version in size 4 yr shown on Amanda (height 38" / 97 cm) and light blue version shown in size 6 yr on Anja (height 47" / 120 cm)
2 (2, 3, 4, 4) (5, 6, 7, 8) skeins of Double Sunday by Sandnes Garn (100% merino wool, 120 yds / 108 m – 50 g), colourways Almond (cream) and Sea Breeze (light blue)

Dark blue version in size 2 yr shown on Arvi (height 28" / 71 cm)
BFL Light DK by The Uncommon Thread (100% Blue Faced Leicester, 246 yds / 224 m – 100 g), colourway Naval Officer

Or 200 (240, 300, 375, 450) (585, 720, 840, 945) yds / 183 (219, 274, 343, 411) (535, 658, 768, 864) m of DK-weight yarn

Needles: US 2 / 2.75 mm 16" / 40 cm circular needles (optional), 24" / 60 cm and a set of DPNs. US 4 / 3.5 mm 16" / 40 cm circular needles (optional), 24" / 60 cm and a set of DPNs

Notions: Stitch markers, waste yarn or stitch holders, tapestry needle, 6 (6, 6, 7, 7) (7, 8, 8, 8) small buttons

GAUGE

22 sts x 30 rows to 4" / 10 cm on US 4 / 3.5 mm needles in St St, after blocking

22 sts x 33 rows to 4" / 10 cm on US 4 / 3.5 mm needles in Broken Garter Ridge St, after blocking

STITCH PATTERNS

BROKEN GARTER RIDGE PATT 1 (WORKED FLAT, MULTIPLE OF 4 STS)
Row 1 (RS): K1, p2, *k2, p2* to last st, k1.
Row 2 (WS): P1, *k2, p2* to last 3 sts, k2, p1.
Row 3 (RS): K.
Row 4 (WS): K.
Rep rows 1–4 for patt.

BROKEN GARTER RIDGE PATT 2 (WORKED IN THE RND, MULTIPLE OF 4 STS)
Rnds 1 and 2: K1, p2, *k2, p2* to last st, k1.
Rnd 3: K.
Rnd 4: P.
Rep rnds 1–4 for patt.

NOTES

Sleeve instructions are written for a set of DPNs. However, an alternate method of working small circumferences, such as Magic-Loop Method or short circular needles, can be used for the larger sizes.

INSTRUCTIONS

The cardigan is worked from the top down with raglan shaping. An all-over textured pattern is worked throughout to add interest.

BODY

NECK BAND
With US 2 / 2.75 mm 24" / 60 cm circular needles, CO 61 (65, 69, 73, 77) (85, 89, 93, 101) sts using the Long-Tail CO Method, or your preferred method. You will cont to work flat.

Row 1: *K1, p1* to last st, k1.
Row 2: P1, *k1, p1* to end.
Rep rows 1 and 2, 2 (2, 2, 2, 2) (2, 3, 3, 3) more times.
Rep row 1 once more. WS is facing for next row.

Change to US 4 / 3.5 mm 24" / 60 cm circular needles.
Adjustment and Set-Up Row: K9 (10, 11, 11, 13) (13, 14, 15, 18) for right front, PM, k1, PM, k10 (10, 10, 10, 10) (12, 12, 12, 12) for right sleeve, PM, k1, PM, k9 (10, 11, 13, 13) (15, 16, 17, 18), k2tog, k8 (9, 10, 12, 12) (14, 15, 16, 17) for back, PM, k1, PM, k10 (10, 10, 10, 10) (12, 12, 12, 12) for left sleeve, PM, k1, PM, k9 (10, 11, 11, 13) (13, 14, 15, 18) for left front . [60 (64, 68, 72, 76) (84, 88, 92, 100) sts] (8 new m's placed, 1 st dec'd)

Est Broken Garter Ridge Patt 1 as foll:
Row 1: K1, p2, *k2, p2* to 2 (3, 0, 0, 2) (2, 3, 0, 3) sts bef first m, k2 (2, 0, 0, 2) (2, 2, 0, 2), p0 (1, 0, 0, 0) (0, 1, 0, 1), SM, k1, SM, k0 (0, 1, 1, 0) (0, 0, 1, 0), p1 (0, 2, 2, 1) (1, 0, 2, 0), *k2, p2* to 1 (2, 3, 3, 1) (3, 0, 1, 0) st(s) bef next m, k1 (2, 2, 2, 1) (2, 0, 1, 0), p0 (0, 1, 1, 0) (1, 0, 0, 0), SM, k1, SM, k0 (0, 0, 0, 0) (0, 1, 0, 1), p2 (1, 0, 0, 2) (0, 2, 2, 2), *k2, p2* to 0 (3, 2, 2, 0) (2, 1, 0, 1) st(s) bef next m, k0 (2, 2, 2, 0) (2, 1, 0, 1), p0 (1, 0, 0, 0) (0, 0, 0, 0), SM, k1, SM, k1 (0, 0, 0, 1) (0, 0, 1, 0), p2 (0, 1, 1, 2) (1, 2, 2, 2), *k2, p2* to 3 (2, 1, 1, 3) (3, 2, 1, 2) st(s) bef next m, k2 (2, 1, 1, 2) (2, 2, 1, 2), p1 (0, 0, 0, 1) (1, 0, 0, 0), SM, k1, SM, p0 (1, 2, 2, 0) (0, 1, 2, 1), *k2, p2* to last st, k1.
Row 2: P1, *k2, p2* to 0 (1, 2, 2, 0) (0, 1, 2, 1) st(s) bef first m, k0 (1, 2, 2, 0) (0, 1, 2, 1), SM, p1, SM, k1 (0, 0, 0, 1) (1, 0, 0, 0), p2 (2, 1, 1, 2) (2, 2, 1, 2), *k2, p2* to 3 (0, 1, 1, 3) (1, 2, 3, 2) st(s) bef next m, k2 (0, 1, 1, 2) (1, 2, 2, 2), p1 (0, 0, 0, 1) (0, 0, 1, 0), SM, p1, SM, k0 (1, 0, 0, 0) (0, 0, 0, 0), p0 (2, 2, 2, 0) (2, 1, 0, 1), *k2, p2* to 2 (1, 0, 0, 2) (0, 3, 2, 3) st(s) bef next m, k2 (1, 0, 0, 2) (0, 2, 2, 2), p0 (0, 0, 0, 0) (0, 1, 0, 1), SM, p1, SM, k0 (0, 1, 1, 0) (1, 0, 0, 0), p1 (2, 2, 2, 1) (2, 0, 1, 0), *k2, p2* to 1 (0, 3, 3, 1) (1, 0, 2, 0) st(s) bef next m, k1 (0, 2, 2, 1) (1, 0, 2, 0), p0 (0, 1, 1, 0) (0, 0, 0, 0), SM, p1, SM, k0 (1, 0, 0, 0) (0, 1, 0, 1), p2 (2, 0, 0, 2) (2, 2, 0, 2), *k2, p2* to last 3 sts, k2, p1.
Row 3: K, slipping all m's.
Row 4: *K to m, SM, p1, SM*, rep *-* 3 more times, k to end.

RAGLAN INCREASES

Rep rows 1–4 for Broken Garter Ridge Patt 1 and at same time, beg raglan inc as foll:

Note! When working Broken Garter Ridge Patt 1 and raglan shaping (use the Stitch Pattern Instructions as a guide), it will not always be possible to complete a full patt rep. Keep to patt as est.
Row 1 (Inc): *Patt as est to next m, m1r, SM, k1, SM, m1l*, rep *-* 3 more times, patt as est to end. (8 sts inc'd)
Row 2: *Patt as est to next m, SM, p1, SM*, rep *-* 3 more times, patt as est to end.

Cont in this manner, that is, working inc row every other row 8 (9, 9, 11, 15) (15, 16, 16, 17) more times, then every 4th row 2 (2, 3, 3, 1) (3, 3, 4, 4) times. [148 (160, 172, 192, 212) (236, 248, 260, 276) sts total: 20 (22, 24, 26, 30) (32, 34, 36, 40) sts for each front, 34 (36, 38, 42, 46) (52, 54, 56, 58) sts for each sleeve (including raglan sts) and 40 (44, 48, 56, 60) (68, 72, 76, 80) sts for back]

Next Row (WS): *Patt as est to next m, SM, p1, SM*, rep *-* 3 more times, patt as est to end.

DIVIDE FOR BODY

Next Row (RS): Patt as est to next m, removing all m's, pl next 34 (36, 38, 42, 46) (52, 54, 56, 58) sts from left sleeve and 2 raglan sts onto waste yarn, using Backwards Loop Method, CO 2 (4, 4, 4, 4) (4, 4, 6, 6) sts for left underarm, patt as est across next 40 (44, 48, 56, 60) (68, 72, 76, 80) sts for back, pl next 34 (36, 38, 42, 46) (52, 54, 56, 58) sts from right sleeve and 2 raglan sts onto waste yarn, using Backwards Loop Method, CO 2 (4, 4, 4, 4) (4, 4, 6, 6) sts for right underarm, patt as est to end. [84 (96, 104, 116, 128) (140, 148, 160, 172) sts]

Cont in Broken Garter Ridge Patt 1 as est until body measures approx. 3.25 (3.75, 4.25, 4.75, 5.25) (6.25, 7, 7.5, 8)" / 8 (10, 11, 12, 13) (16, 18, 19, 20) cm from underarm or 0.75 (0.75, 0.75, 0.75, 0.75) (0.75, 1, 1, 1)" / 2 (2, 2, 2, 2) (2, 3, 3, 3) cm less than desired length to start of lower hem ending with a row 3 of Garter Ridge Patt 1. WS is facing for next row.

Next Row: K, inc 1 st at centre back using an m1l. [85 (97, 105, 117, 129) (141, 149, 161, 173) sts]

LOWER HEM
With US 2 / 2.75 mm 24" / 60 cm circular needles, work as foll:
Row 1: *K1, p1* to last st, k1.

Row 2: P1, *k1, p1* to end.
Rep rows 1 and 2, 2 (2, 2, 2, 2) (2, 3, 3, 3) more times.
BO evenly in rib patt as est.

SLEEVES

Pl 34 (36, 38, 42, 46) (52, 54, 56, 58) sts on waste yarn for right sleeve onto US 4 / 3.5 mm set of DPNs or preferred style for working small circumferences. Beg at centre of underarm, pick up and k 1 (2, 2, 2, 2) (2, 2, 3, 3) st(s) along underarm CO sts, patt as est across the 34 (36, 38, 42, 46) (52, 54, 56, 58) sts from sleeve, and then pick up and k 1 (2, 2, 2, 2) (2, 2, 3, 3) st(s) along underarm CO to centre. PM for BOR. [36 (40, 42, 46, 50) (56, 58, 62, 64) sts]

Beg with the appropriate row of patt, cont to work in Broken Garter Ridge Patt 2 as est in the rnd (using Stitch Pattern instructions as a guide) until 15 (11, 11, 11, 9) (9, 9, 9, 9) rnds have been completed.

Dec Rnd: Work 1 st in patt as est, work a k2tog/p2tog decrease, work in patt as est to 3 sts from end, work 2tog, work last st in patt as est. (2 sts dec'd)

Working in Broken Garter Ridge Patt 2 as est, rep dec rnd every 16th (8th, 8th, 10th, 8th) (8th, 12th, 10th, 12th) rnd 1 (3, 4, 4, 6) (7, 6, 8, 7) more time(s). [32 (32, 32, 36, 36) (40, 44, 44, 48) sts]

If necessary, work in patt as est until sleeve measures 5 (5.25, 6.25, 7.25, 7.75) (9, 10.5, 12, 13)" / 13 (13, 16, 18, 19) (23, 26, 30, 33) cm or 0.75 (0.75, 0.75, 0.75, 0.75) (0.75, 1, 1, 1)" / 2 (2, 2, 2, 2) (2, 3, 3, 3) cm less than desired length to start of sleeve cuff ending with a p row or a row 4 of Broken Garter Ridge Patt 2.

SLEEVE CUFF

With US 2 / 2.75 mm set of DPNs or preferred style for working small circumferences, work as foll:
Rnd 1: *K1, p1* to end.
Rep rnd 1, 5 (5, 5, 5, 5) (5, 7, 7, 7) more times.
BO evenly in 1 x 1 rib patt.
Work second sleeve as first.

BUTTON BANDS

LEFT FRONT BUTTON BAND
With RS facing, US 2 / 2.75 mm 24" / 60 cm circular needles, pick up and k 60 (66, 70, 78, 82) (94, 104, 108, 112) sts evenly down left front edge (approx. 3 sts for every 4 rows).
Row 1: *K1, p1* to end.
Rep row 1, 4 (4, 4, 4, 4) (4, 6, 6, 6) more times.
BO evenly in 1 x 1 rib patt.

RIGHT FRONT BUTTONHOLE BAND
Sizes 0–3 mos, 3–6 mos, 6–12 mos, 12–18 mos, 2 yr and 4 yr only
With RS facing, US 2 / 2.75 mm 24" / 60 cm circular needles, pick up and k sts as bef, evenly up right front edge and ending with same number of sts as for button band.

Row 1: *K1, p1* to end.
Rep row 1 once more.
Next Row (make buttonholes): K1, p1, *k2tog, yo, (k1, p1) 4 (5, 5, 5, 5) (6, –, –, –) times*, rep *–* 4 (4, 4, 5, 5) (5, –, –, –) more times, k2tog, yo, *k1, p1* 3 (1, 3, 1, 3) (3, –, –, –) time(s).
Rep row 1, 2 more times.
BO evenly in 1 x 1 rib patt.

Sizes 6 yr, 8 yr, and 10 yr only
With RS facing, US 2 / 2.75 mm 24" / 60 cm circular needles, pick up and k sts as bef, evenly up right front edge and ending with same number of sts as for button band.

Row 1: *K1, p1* to end.
Rep row 1, 2 more times.
Next Row (make buttonholes): *K1, p1* – (–, –, –, –) (–, 1, 3, 5) time(s), *k2tog, yo, (k1, p1) – (–, –, –, –) (–, 6, 6, 6) times*, rep *–* 6 more times, k2tog, yo, k1, p1.
Rep row 1, 3 more times. BO evenly in 1 x 1 rib patt.

FINISHING

Weave in ends, closing any gaps that remain at the underarms. Sew buttons to correspond to buttonholes on the left front button band. Block to measurements.

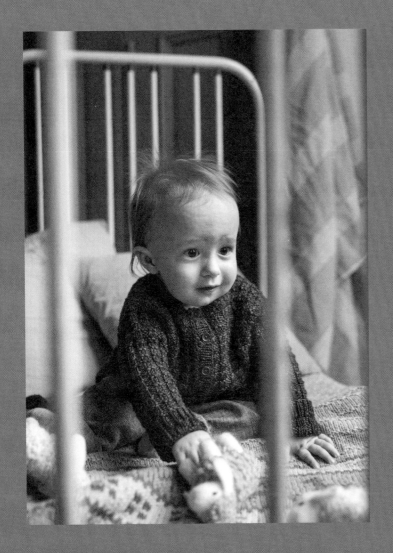

hello,
little lamb!

ALEX

**I named this sweater after my younger brother, Alex.
It is an easy everyday knit with rustic details.**

SIZES

0–6 mos (6–12 mos, 12–18 mos, 2 yr) (4 yr, 6 yr, 8 yr, 10 yr)
Recommended ease: 2" / 5 cm of positive ease
Shown in size 4 yr on Ilana (height 38" / 97 cm)

FINISHED MEASUREMENTS

Chest Circumference: 18 (20, 22.25, 24.25) (26, 28, 30.25, 32.25)" / 45 (50, 56, 60) (65, 70, 76, 80) cm
Body Length to Underarm: 4.5 (5, 6, 7.5) (9, 10, 11, 11.5)" / 11 (13, 15, 19) (23, 25, 28, 29) cm
Raglan Depth: 4.25 (4.75, 5.25, 5.25) (6.25, 6.5, 7, 7.25)" / 11 (12, 13, 13) (16, 16, 18, 18) cm
Upper Arm Circumference: 6.75 (8, 8.5, 9.25) (10.25, 10.75, 11, 11.5)" / 17 (20, 21, 23) (26, 27, 28, 29) cm
Sleeve Length to Underarm: 6 (7, 8, 8.5) (10, 11.5, 13, 14)" / 15 (18, 20, 21) (25, 29, 33, 35) cm

MATERIALS

Yarn: 1 (1, 1, 2) (2, 2, 3, 3) skein(s) of Semilla Pura by BC Garn (100% GOTS certified organic wool-weight, 382 yds / 350 m – 100 g), colourway Beige Gray Marled 04
Or 211 (266, 317, 370) (473, 543, 953, 1048) yds / 193 (244, 290, 339) (433, 497, 872, 959) m of DK-weight yarn

Needles: US 2 / 2.75 mm 16" / 40 cm circular needles, 24" / 60 cm circular needles (for sizes 4–10 yrs) and a set of DPNs. US 4 / 3.5 mm 16" / 40 cm circular needles (for 4 smallest sizes), 24" / 60 cm circular needles (for sizes 4–10 yrs) and a set of DPNs

Notions: 7 Stitch markers (1 of a different colour for BOR and 2 of another colour for centre front charts), waste yarn or stitch holders, tapestry needle, 1 small button (for 4 smallest sizes)

GAUGE

21 sts x 32 rows to 4" / 10 cm on US 4 / 3.5 mm needles in St St, after blocking

NOTES

Sleeve instructions are written for a set of DPNs. However, an alternate method of working small circumferences, such as Magic-Loop Method or short circular needles, can be used for the larger sizes. As the raglan shaping increases, change to longer circular needles when necessary.

A simple knit and purl stitch is worked in the rnd from charts on the front of the sweater. The charts are read from bottom to top and from right to left when knitting in the rnd.

INSTRUCTIONS

The pullover is worked from the top down with raglan shaping. A small section of short rows is worked at the bottom of the back raglan shaping for a more comfortable fit. A button closure at the back of the neck is included for the 4 smallest sizes.

BODY

NECK EDGE
Sizes 0–6 mos, 6–12 mos, 12–18 mos and 2 yr only
With US 2 / 2.75 mm set of DPNs or 16" / 40 cm circular needles, CO 76 (78, 78, 84) (–, –, –, –) sts using the Long-Tail CO Method, or your preferred method. Do not join in the rnd.
Working back and forth on the circular needle, p 1 row.
Next Row: K2, yo, k2tog (buttonhole made), k to end.
Next Row: P.
Next Row (WS): BO 6 sts pwise for button tab, p to end, turn. RS is facing. Join in rnd. Pl BOR m (centre back neck). [70 (72, 72, 78) (–, –, –, –) sts]

Sizes 4 yr, 6 yr, 8 yr and 10 yr only
With US 2 / 2.75 mm set of DPNs or 16" / 40 cm circular needles, CO – (–, –, –) (80, 82, 82, 92) sts using the Long-Tail CO Method, or your preferred method. Join in the rnd making sure sts are not twisted. PM for BOR (centre back neck).
Rnd 1: *K1, p1* to end.
Work in 1 x 1 rib as est until work measures 0.75" / 2 cm.

All sizes resume
Change to US 4 / 3.5 mm 16" / 40 cm circular needles or preferred style for working small circumferences (set of DPNs for 2 smallest sizes).

Set-Up Rnd: M1l, k11 (11, 12, 13) (13, 14, 15, 17), PM, k1, PM, k10 (11, 9, 10) (11, 10, 8, 9), PM, k1, PM, k0 (0, 1, 0) (0, 1, 2, 4), work rnd 1 from Chart A (A, A, B) (B, B, B, B), k0 (0, 1, 0) (0, 1, 2, 4), PM, k1, PM, k10 (11, 9, 10) (11, 10, 8, 9), PM, k1, PM, k12 (12, 13, 14) (14, 15, 16, 18). [71 (73, 73, 79) (81, 83, 83, 93) sts total: 23 (23, 25, 27) (27, 29, 31, 35) sts for front, 24 (24, 26, 28) (28, 30, 32, 36) sts for back, 10 (11, 9, 10) (11, 10, 8, 9) sts for each sleeve and 4 sts between raglan m's]

RAGLAN INCREASES
Change to 24" / 60 cm circular needle when necessary.

Rnd 1: *K to m, m1r, SM, k1, SM, m1l*, rep *–* once more, k0 (0, 1, 0) (0, 1, 2, 4), PM for chart, work rnd 2 from Chart A (A, A, B) (B, B, B, B), PM for chart, k0 (0, 1, 0) (0, 1, 2, 4), m1r, SM, k1, SM, m1l, k to m, m1r, SM, k1, SM, m1l, k to end. (8 sts inc'd)
Rnd 2: K to chart m, SM, work rnd 3 from Chart A (A, A, B) (B, B, B, B), SM, k to end.
Rnd 3 (Inc): *K to m, m1r, SM, k1, SM, m1l*, rep *–* once more, k to m, SM, work appropriate rnd from Chart A (A, A, B) (B, B, B, B), SM, *k to m, m1r, SM, k1, SM, m1l*, rep *–* once more, k to end. (8 sts inc'd)
Rnd 4: K to chart m, SM, work appropriate rnd from Chart A (A, A, B) (B, B, B, B), SM, k to end.
Rep rnd 3 (inc rnd) every other rnd 3 (5, 7, 9) (9, 9, 11, 9) more times, then every 4th rnd, 5 (5, 5, 4) (6, 7, 6, 8) more times, and at same time, work appropriate rnd from Chart A (A, A, B) (B, B, B, B) between m's. [151 (169, 185, 199) (217, 227, 235, 245) sts]

Note! Once the 24 (24, 24, 28) (28, 28, 28, 28) rnds of chart have been completed, remove the chart m's and cont to knit the front sts between the raglan m's instead.

K 3 (3, 3, 3) (3, 1, 5, 2) rnds.

BACK YOKE SHAPING
Short Row 1 (RS): K to 2 (2, 3, 3) (3, 5, 5, 5) sts bef raglan m, w&t.
Short Row 2 (WS): P to BOR, SM, p to 2 (2, 3, 3) (3, 5, 5, 5) sts bef raglan m, w&t.
Short Row 3 (RS): Slipping BOR, k to 3 (3, 4, 4) (4, 6, 6, 6) sts from previously wrapped st, PUW, w&t.

Short Row 4 (WS): Slipping BOR, p to 3 (3, 4, 4) (4, 6, 6, 6) sts from previously wrapped st, PUW, w&t.
Rep short rows 3–4, 0 (0, 0, 1) (1, 1, 1, 1) more time.
Sizes 6 yr, 8 yr and 10 yr only
Next Short Row (RS): Slipping m, k to – (–, –, –) (–, 7, 7, 7) sts from wrapped st, PUW, w&t.
Next Short Row (WS): Slipping m, p to – (–, –, –) (–, 7, 7, 7) sts from wrapped st, PUW, w&t.
Next Rnd (RS): K to BOR, SM, k 1 rnd working final wraps sts in same manner.

All sizes resume
DIVIDE FOR BODY
Next Rnd: K to m, RM, pl next 32 (37, 39, 42) (47, 48, 48, 49) sts from left sleeve and 2 raglan sts on to waste yarn or st holder, RM, using the Backwards Loop Method, CO 4 (5, 5, 6) (7, 8, 10, 11) sts, k across front sts to next m, RM, pl next 32 (37, 39, 42) (47, 48, 48, 49) sts from left sleeve and 2 raglan sts on to waste yarn or st holder, RM, using the Backwards Loop Method, CO 4 (5, 5, 6) (7, 8, 10, 11) sts, k to end. [95 (105, 117, 127) (137, 147, 159, 169) sts]

Cont in St St in the rnd until body measures 3.5 (4, 5, 6.5) (8, 9, 10, 10.5)" / 9 (10, 13, 16) (20, 23, 25, 26) cm from underarm or 1" / 2.5 cm less than desired length to start of lower hem.

HEM
With US 2 / 2.75 mm 24" / 60 cm circular needles, work as foll:
Rnd 1: Ssk, p1, *k1, p1* to end. (1 st dec'd)
Rnd 2: *K1, p1* to end.
Cont in est 1 x 1 rib until work measures 1" / 2.5 cm
BO evenly in 1 x 1 rib patt.

SLEEVES

Pl 32 (37, 39, 42) (47, 48, 48, 49) on waste yarn for right sleeve onto US 4 / 3.5 mm set of DPNs or preferred style for working small circumferences, and beg at centre of underarm, pick up and k 2 (2, 2, 3) (3, 4, 5, 5) sts along underarm CO sts, k32 (37, 39, 42) (47, 48, 48, 49) sts from sleeve, and then pick up and k 2 (3, 3, 3) (4, 4, 5, 6) sts along underarm CO to centre. PM for BOR. [36 (42, 44, 48) (54, 56, 58, 60) sts]

Work 5 (5, 5, 5) (5, 7, 7, 7) rnds in St St.

Dec Rnd: K1, ssk, k to last 3 sts, k2tog, k1. (2 sts dec'd)

Rep dec rnd every 6th (6th, 6th, 6th) (6th, 8th, 8th, 8th) rnd 3 (3, 6, 7) (7, 3, 8, 10) more times, the every – (4th, –, –) (4th, 6th, 6th, 6th) rnd – (3, –, –) (3, 7, 2, 1) more time(s). [28 (28, 30, 32) (32, 34, 36, 36) sts]

Cont in St St in the rnd until sleeve measures 5 (6, 7, 7.5) (9, 10.5, 12, 13)" / 13 (15, 18, 19) (23, 26, 30, 33) cm from underarm or 1" / 2.5 cm less than desired length.

CUFF

With US 2 / 2.75 mm set of DPNs, work as foll:

Rnd 1: *K1, p1* to end.

Cont in est 1 x 1 rib for 1" / 2.5 cm.

BO evenly in 1 x 1 rib patt.

Work second sleeve as first.

FINISHING

Weave in ends, closing any gaps that remain at the underarms. Sizes 0–6 mos, 6–12 mos, 12–18 mos and 2 yr sew button to correspond to buttonhole on neckband. Block to measurements.

WRITTEN INSTRUCTIONS FOR CHARTS

CHART A (WORKED OVER 23 STS)

Rnds 1–2: P1, k5, p1, k9, p1, k5, p1.

Rnds 3–4: K1, p1, k5, p1, k7, p1, k5, p1, k1.

Rnds 5–6: K2, *p1, k5*, rep *–* twice more, p1, k2.

Rnds 7–8: *K3, p1, k5, p1*, rep *–* once more, k3.

Rnds 9–10: K4, p1, k5, p1, k1, p1, k5, p1, k4.

Rnds 11–12: *K5, p1*, rep *–* twice more, k5.

Rnds 13–14: K6, p1, k9, p1, k6.

Rnds 15–16: *K7, p1*, rep *–* once more, k7.

Rnds 17–18: K8, p1, k5, p1, k8.

Rnds 19–20: K9, p1, k3, p1, k9.

Rnds 21–22: K10, p1, k1, p1, k10.

Rnds 23–24: K11, p1, k11.

CHART B (WORKED OVER 27 STS)

Rnds 1–2: P1, k6, p1, k11, p1, k6, p1.

Rnds 3–4: K1, p1, k6, p1, k9, p1, k6, p1, k1.

Rnds 5–6: K2, p1, k6, p1, k7, p1, k6, p1, k2.

Rnds 7–8: K3, p1, k6, p1, k5, p1, k6, p1, k3.

Rnds 9–10: K4, p1, k6, p1, k3, p1, k6, p1, k4.

Rnds 11–12: K5, p1, k6, p1, k1, p1, k6, p1, k5.

Rnds 13–14: *K6, p1*, rep *–* twice more, k6.

Rnds 15–16: K7, p1, k11, p1, k7.

Rnds 17–18: K8, p1, k9, p1, k8.

Rnds 19–20: K9, p1, k7, p1, k9.

Rnds 21–22: K10, p1, k5, p1, k10.

Rnds 23–24: K11, p1, k3, p1, k11.

Rnds 25–26: K12, p1, k1, p1, k12.

Rnds 27–28: K13, p1, k13.

CHART A
Sizes 0–6, 6–12 and 12–18 mos only

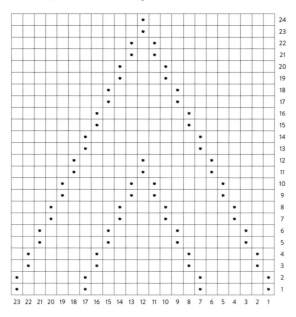

knit

• purl

CHART B
Sizes 2, 4, 6, 8 and 10 yrs only

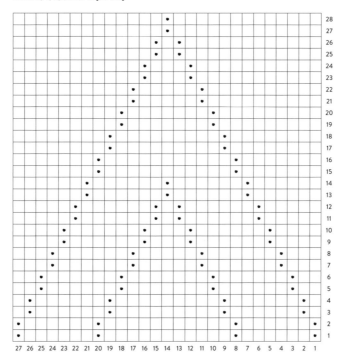

I got the idea for these socks from the blue seas of Barcelona.
They are knit with mohair and sock yarn held together,
making them so soft and warm — like fine sand on the beach.

BARCELONA

SIZES

0–6 mos (6–12 mos, 1–2 yrs, 2–5 yrs) (5–7 yrs, 7+ yrs)

FINISHED MEASUREMENTS

Foot Circumference: 4.25 (5, 5.5, 6.25) (6.75, 7.5)" / 11 (13, 14, 16) (17, 17) cm
Leg Height: 5 (6.5, 7.5, 8.5) (9.5, 10.5)" / 13 (16, 19, 21) (24, 26) cm
Foot Length: 3.5 (4, 5, 6) (7, 8)" / 9 (11, 12, 15) (18, 20) cm

MATERIALS

Yarn:
Blue version
Yarn A: 1 skein of Fingering Weight Merino by Kokon (100% merino, 349 yds / 320 m – 100 g), colourway Cloud

Yarn B: 1 skein of Kidsilk Mohair by Kokon Kidsilk Mohair (72% kid mohair, 28% silk, 229 yds / 209 m – 25 g), colourway Blue Moon

Yellow version
Yarn A: 1 skein of Sock Yarn by Isager (40% easy wash alpaca, 40% easy wash merino, 20% recycled nylon, 419 yds / 384 m – 100 g), colourway 22

Yarn B: 1 ball of Silk Mohair by Isager (75% kid mohair, 25% silk, 232 yds / 212 m – 25 g), colourway 22

Or 61 (88, 110, 148) (181, 225) yds / 55 (80, 100, 135) (165, 205) m of fingering-weight yarn and 61 (88, 110, 148) (181, 225) yds / 55 (80, 100, 135) (165, 205) m of lace-weight yarn

Both yarns are held together throughout the pattern.

Needles: US 1.5 / 2.5 mm set of DPNs and US 2 / 2.75 mm set of DPNs

Notions: Removable stitch markers, stitch holder or waste yarn, tapestry needle

GAUGE

26 sts x 50 rows to 4" / 10 cm on US 2 / 2.75 mm needles in St St with yarns A and B held together, after blocking

NOTES

Instructions are written for DPNs. However, an alternate method of working small circumferences, such as Magic-Loop Method, can be used. If using Magic-Loop Method, place a marker for each needle change when setting up gusset. Foot length is adjustable.

The chart is read from bottom to top and from right to left when knitting in the rnd.

INSTRUCTIONS

The socks are worked from the cuff down to the toe. The heel is shaped using the heel flap method. The toe is grafted together.

CUFF

Using US 1.5 / 2.5 mm set of DPNs and a strand each of yarns A and B held together, CO 28 (32, 36, 40) (44, 48) sts with Long-Tail CO Method, or your preferred method. Evenly distribute sts over 4 DPNs. Join in the rnd making sure sts are not twisted. Pl a removable m for BOR.

Rnd 1: *K2, p2* to end.
Work in 2 x 2 rib as est until work measures 1" / 2.5 cm from CO edge or to desired length.
Change to US 2 / 2.75 mm set of DPNs.

LEG

Rnd 1: K.
Rep rnd 1, 8 more times.

Next Rnd: K to end, m1l, SM. [29, (33, 37, 41) (45, 49) sts]

Beg working from chart as folls:
Rnd 1: K14 (17, 20, 23) (26, 29), PM, work rnd 1 of chart, PM, k to end.

Rnd 2: K to m, SM, work rnd 2 of chart, SM, k to end. *Note!* For size 0–6 mos, second m is BOR.

Cont as est, working chart until 23 rnds of chart have been completed and removing m's except BOR on last rnd.
Next Rnd: K to 2 sts bef BOR, K2tog. [28, (32, 36, 40) (44, 48) sts]

Work in St St in the rnd until work measures 5 (6.5, 7.5, 8.5) (9.5, 10.5)" / 13 (16, 19, 21) (24, 26) cm or desired length from CO edge.

HEEL FLAP
K14 (16, 18, 20) (22, 24). These sts will not be worked again until heel is complete.
Row 1 (RS): *Sl1 pwise, k1* to end.
Turn work so that WS is facing you, removing BOR m.
Next Row (WS): Sl1 pwise, p13 (15, 17, 19) (21, 23).
Divide these 14 (16, 18, 20) (22, 24) sts onto 2 DPNs.

Cont to work back and forth in rows on the 14 (16, 18, 20) (22, 24) sts to form heel flap as folls:
Row 1 (RS): *Sl1 pwise, k1* to end.
Row 2 (WS): Sl1 pwise, p13 (15, 17, 19) (21, 23).
Rep rows 1 and 2, 5 (6, 7, 8) (9, 10) more times

TURN HEEL
Working on the 14 (16, 18, 20) (22, 24) sts, cont as folls:
Row 1 (RS): Sl1 pwise, k8 (8, 8, 11) (12, 12), ssk, k1, turn.
Row 2 (WS): Sl1 pwise, p3 (3, 3, 5) (5, 5), p2tog, p1, turn.
Row 3 (RS): Sl1 pwise, k4 (4, 4, 6) (6, 6), ssk, k1, turn.
Row 4 (WS): Sl1 pwise, p5 (5, 5, 7) (7, 7), p2tog, p1, turn.
Cont to work back and forth in rows in this manner, closing the gaps as est until all of the sts have been worked. You will end after a WS row. [8 (10, 12, 12) (14, 16) sts]

RE-ESTABLISH WORKING IN THE RND
Next Rnd (RS): K4 (5, 6, 6) (7, 8) heel sts. With an empty needle (N1) k rem 4 (5, 6, 6) (7, 8) sts. With the same needle, pick up and k7 (8, 9, 10) (11, 12) sts along edge of heel flap, working into the sl sts. With a second needle (N2), k7 (8, 9, 10) (11, 12) sts from the instep, then with a third needle (N3), k7 (8, 9, 10) (11, 12) sts rem for instep. With a fourth needle (N4), pick up and k7 (8, 9, 10) (11, 12) sts along other side of heel flap, working into sl sts.

With the same needle, k4 (5, 6, 6) (7, 8) sts from heel. Pl BOR m (centre of heel). [36 (42, 48, 52) (58, 64) sts]

K 1 rnd.

GUSSET SHAPING
Rnd 1: N1 – K to last 3 sts, k2tog, k1. N2 and N3 – K. N4 – K1, ssk, k to end. (2 sts dec'd)
Rnd 2: K.
Rep rnds 1 and 2, 4 (5, 6, 6) (7, 8) times total. [28, (32, 36, 40) (44, 48) sts]

Work in St St in the rnd until work measures approx. 2.5 (3, 3.75, 4.75) (5.5, 6.5)" / 6 (8, 9, 12) (14, 16) cm from back of heel or 1 (1, 1.25, 1.25) (1.5, 1.5)" / 3 (3, 3, 3) (4, 4) cm less than desired foot length.

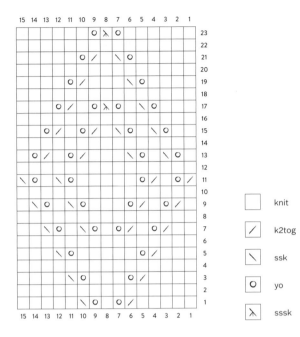

Legend:
- □ knit
- ╱ k2tog
- ╲ ssk
- ○ yo
- 入 sssk

TOE SHAPING

Next Rnd: K.

Dec Rnd 1: N1 – K to last 3 sts, k2tog, k1. N2 – K1, ssk, k to end. N3 – K to last 3 sts, k2tog, k1. N4 – K1, ssk, k to end. (4 sts dec'd)

Rnd 2: K.

Rep rnds 1 and 2, 4 (5, 6, 6) (7, 8) more times, working last rnd as folls:

Last Rnd: N1 – K. N2 – K. N3 – Using N2, k all N3 sts. N4 – K. N1 – Using N4, k all N1 sts. [8 (8, 8, 12) (12, 12) sts] [with 4 (4, 4, 6) (6, 6) sts on each of 2 rem needles]

FINISHING

Break yarn leaving an 8″ / 20 cm long tail. Thread tail through tapestry needle and graft 4 (4, 4, 6) (6, 6) sts on each needle tog.
Work second sock as first.
Weave in ends and block to measurements.

CATHEDRAL

Cathedral got its name from the intricate spires seen on gothic and neo-gothic cathedrals. While it may take a bit longer to make this sweater than the other projects in the book, the result is a timeless, comfortable yet dressy knit for more important occasions.

SIZES

6–12 mos (12–18 mos, 2 yr, 4 yr) (6 yr, 8 yr, 10 yr)
Recommended ease: 2–4" / 5–10 cm of positive ease
at chest

FINISHED MEASUREMENTS

Chest Circumference: 20.75 (22.25, 23.5, 25.75) (27.75,
29, 30.25)" / 52 (56, 59, 64) (69, 73, 76) cm
Yoke Depth (front): 4.5 (4.75, 5, 6) (6.25, 6.75, 7)" / 12
(13, 13, 15) (16, 17, 17.75) cm
Body Length to Underarm (front): 7.5 (8, 9, 10) (10.5, 11,
11.5)" / 19 (20.25, 23, 25.5) (26.5, 28, 29.25) cm
Upper Arm Circumference: 7.25 (7.5, 8, 8.75) (10, 10.5,
11)" / 18 (19, 20, 22) (25, 26, 27) cm
Sleeve Length to Underarm: 7.5 (8.5, 9, 10.5) (11.5, 13,
14)" / 19 (21.5, 23, 26.5) (29, 33, 35) cm

MATERIALS

Yarn:
White version shown on Amanda (height 38" / 97 cm)
2 (2, 3, 3) (4, 4, 4) skeins of Kid Classic by Rowan (70%
lambswool, 22% kid mohair, 8% polyamide, 153 yds /
140 m – 50 g), colourway Feather
Or 266 (304, 342, 425) (492, 546, 603) yds / 244 (278,
313, 389) (450, 500, 552) m of worsted-weight yarn

Red version shown on Anja (height 47" / 120 cm)
Yarn A: 1 (1, 1, 2) (2, 2, 3) skein(s) of Highland by Isager
(100% wool, 305 yds / 278 m – 50 g), colourway Chili
Or 215 (250, 280, 425) (500, 570, 625) yds / 224 (228,
256, 388) (457, 521, 571) m worsted-weight yarn
Yarn B: 1 (2, 2, 2) (3, 3, 3) skein(s) of Soft Silk Mohair by
Knitting for Olive (70% mohair, 30% silk, 246 yds / 225 m
– 25 g), colourway Forest Berry
Or 215 (250, 280, 425) (500, 570, 625) yds / 224 (228,
256, 388) (457, 521, 571) m of lace-weight yarn

Both yarns are held together throughout the pattern.

Needles: US 6 / 4 mm 16" / 40 cm circular needles and
a set of DPNs. US 7 / 4.5 mm 16" / 40 cm, 24" / 60 cm
circular needles and a set of DPNs

Notions: Stitch markers, stitch holders or waste yarn,
tapestry needle, 1 button for 2 smallest sizes only

GAUGE

19 sts x 24 rnds to 4" / 10 cm on US 7 / 4.5 mm needles
in St St with single strand worsted or with yarns A and B
held together, after blocking

NOTES

This pattern can be worked with a single strand of
worsted-weight yarn or a strand of each fingering and
lace-weight yarn held together throughout.

Sleeve instructions are written for DPNs. However,
an alternate method of working small circumferences,
such as Magic-Loop Method or short circular needles,
can be used. As the yoke decreases, change to shorter
circular needles or DPNs when necessary. Two smallest
sizes have a button closure at back neck. Row gauge is
important to obtain the correct yoke depth.

Charts are read from bottom to top and from right to left
when knitting in the rnd.

SPECIAL ABBREVIATIONS

Twisted Ssk (twisted left decrease): Sl 1 pwise to right
needle, k1, psso (1 st dec'd)

Twisted K2tog (twisted right decrease): Sl 1 pwise to
right needle, sl next st kwise to right needle, sl both sts
back to left needle, k2tog (1 st dec'd)

Twisted CDD (twisted central double decrease): Sl 1
pwise, sl next st as if to p1tbl, return both to left needle,
sl 2tog kwise, k1, p2sso (2 sts dec'd)

INSTRUCTIONS

The pullover is worked from the bottom up with circular
yoke with either a single strand of worsted-weight
yarn or a strand of each fingering and lace-weight
held together throughout. The body and sleeves are
worked separately in the round to the base of the yoke,
then joined to work the yoke. A section of short rows
is worked at the back hem for a more comfortable fit.
Find instructions for the crochet collar, originally
designed for Cielo, shown on p. 104 on pp. 156–157.

take me
with you!

SLEEVES

Using US 8 / 4 mm DPNs, CO 21 (24, 24, 27, 30, 30, 33) sts with the Long-Tail CO Method, or your preferred method. Disperse sts over 4 DPNs. Join in the rnd making sure sts are not twisted. PM for BOR.

Rnd 1: *K1tbl, p2* to end.
Work in 1 x 2 twisted rib patt as est until work measures 1 (1, 1, 1.5) (1.5, 1.5, 1.5)" / 2.5 (2.5, 2.5, 4) (4, 4, 4) cm from CO edge, inc 1 (0, 2, 1) (0, 2, 1) st(s) evenly spaced across last rnd. [22 (24, 26, 28) (30, 32, 34) sts]

Change to US 7 / 4.5 mm DPNs and k 5 rnds.

SLEEVE INCREASES

Inc Rnd: K1, m1l, k to 1 st bef BOR m, m1r, k1. (2 sts inc'd)
Rep inc rnd every 5th (6th, 6th, 6th) (6th, 6th, 8th) rnd 5 (5, 4, 4, 8, 4, 8) more times, then every 0 (0, 8th, 8th) (0, 8th, 0) rnd 0 (0, 1, 2) (0, 4, 0) more time(s). [34 (36, 38, 42) (48, 50, 52) sts]

Work in St St in the rnd until sleeve measures 7.5 (8.5, 9, 10.5) (11.5, 13, 14)" / 19 (21.5, 22.5, 26.5) (29, 32.5, 35) cm from CO edge, or desired length to underarm.

Next Rnd: K, ending 2 sts before BOR m. Pl next 4 sts on waste yarn or st holder for underarm, removing m when you come to it. [30 (32, 34, 38) (44, 46, 48) sts]

Set aside first sleeve, pl rem 30 (32, 34, 38) (44, 46, 48) sts on waste yarn or spare needle.
Work second sleeve as first.

BODY

Using US 8 / 4 mm 16" / 40 cm circular needle, CO 96 (105, 111, 120) (132, 138, 144) sts using the Long-Tail CO Method, or your preferred method. Join in the rnd making sure sts are not twisted. PM for BOR.

Rnd 1: *K1tbl, p2* to end.
Work in 1 x 2 twisted rib patt as est until work measures 1 (1, 1, 1.5) (1.5, 1.5, 1.5)" / 2.5 (2.5, 2.5, 4) (4, 4, 4) cm from CO edge, inc 2 (1, 1, 2) (0, 0, 0) st(s) evenly spaced across last rnd. [98 (106, 112, 122) (132, 138, 144) sts]

Change to US 7 / 4.5 mm 16" / 40 cm circular needle (or longer for child sizes) and work as folls:
Next Rnd: K49 (53, 56, 61) (66, 69, 72), PM for side seam, k to end.

WORK BACK SHORT ROWS

Short Row 1 (RS): K to side m, SM, k6, w&t.
Short Row 2 (WS): P to BOR, sl BOR m, p6, w&t.
Short Row 3 (RS): K to 3 sts bef wrapped st, w&t.
Short Row 4 (WS): P to 3 sts bef wrapped st, w&t.
Rep short rows 3 and 4, 0 (0, 0, 0) (0, 1, 1) more time.

Next Rnd (RS): K around, slipping side m and concealing wrapped sts as you come to them as foll: Sl the RHN under the wrap and k it tog with the st that it wraps. [98 (106, 112, 122) (132, 138, 144) sts]

Work in St St in the rnd until work measures 7.5 (8, 9, 10) (10.5, 11, 11.5)" / 19 (20.25, 23, 25.5) (26.5, 28, 29.25) cm from front CO edge or desired length to underarm and ending 2 sts bef BOR m.

JOIN FOR YOKE

Next Rnd: K next 4 sts, then pl these sts on waste yarn for right underarm, removing BOR m. K across back sts to 2 sts bef side m, pl next 4 sts on waste yarn for underarm, RM. Transfer sts from first sleeve on to left needle of body, and k30 (32, 34, 38) (44, 46, 48) sts for left sleeve, then k across front sts to end. Transfer sts from second sleeve on to left needle of body and k30 (32, 34, 38) (44, 46, 48) sts for right sleeve. PM for new BOR (right back shoulder). [150 (162, 172, 190) (212, 222, 232) sts]

K 1 (3, 4, 0) (2, 4, 6) rnd(s).

Sizes 6–12 mos and 10 yr only
Dec Rnd: K7 (–, –, –) (–, –, 15), *k2tog, k13 (–, –, –) (–, –, 27)* to last 8 (–, –, –) (–, –, 14) sts, k2tog, k6 (–, –, –) (–, –, 12). [140 (–, –, –) (–, –, 224) sts]

Sizes 12–18 mos only
Dec Rnd: K2, *k2tog, k18* to end. [154 sts]

Sizes 2 yr and 6 yr only
Dec Rnd: K all, dec – (–, 4, –) (2, –, –) sts evenly spaced around. [– (–, 168, –) (210, –, –) sts]

Sizes 4 yr and 8 yr only
Dec Rnd: K3, *k2tog, k– (–, –, 21) (–, 16, –)* to last 3 sts, k3. [– (–, –, 182) (–, 210, –) sts]

All sizes resume
Switch to US 7 / 4.5 mm 16" / 40 cm circular needle.
Beg working charts in order as folls, changing to DPNs or Magic-Loop as necessary:

Sizes 6–12 mos, 12–18 mos and 2 yr only
Work Chart A, rnds 1–6 only. (20 sts per rep rem)

Sizes 4 yr, 6 yr, 8 yr and 10 yr only
Work Chart A, rnds 1–10. (14 sts per rep rem)
Rep Chart A, rnds 1–6 only. (20 sts per rep rem)

All sizes resume
Work Chart B, rnds 17–20. (8 sts per rep rem)
Work Chart C, rnds 21–28. (8 sts per rep rem)
Rep Chart C, rnds 21–26 only. (14 sts per rep remain)
Work Chart D, rnds 35–36. (6 sts per rep rem) [60 (66, 72, 78) (90, 90, 96) sts]

Size 6–12 mos only
Dec Rnd: K, dec 3 sts evenly spaced around. [57 sts]

Sizes 12–18 mos, 2 yr, 8 yr and 10 yr only
Dec Rnd: K– (5, 3, –) (–, 2, 2) *k2tog, k– (9, 6, –) (–, 3, 2)* to last – (6, 5, –) (–, 3, 2) sts, k2tog, k– (4, 3, –) (–, 1, 0). [– (60, 63, –) (–, 72, 72) sts]

Size 4 yr only
Dec Rnd: K3, *k2tog, k4, k2tog, k5* to last 10 sts, k2tog, k4, k2tog, k2. [66 sts]

Size 6 yr only
Dec Rnd: K3, *k2tog, k2* to last sts, k3. [69 sts]

NECKBAND

Sizes 6–12 mos and 12–18 mos only
Change to US 8 / 4 mm 16" / 40 cm circular needle and work back and forth as folls:
Row 1 (WS): Turn work so that WS is facing, *p1, k2* to end, using the Backwards Loop Method, CO 4 sts. [61 (64, –, –) (–, –, –) sts]
Row 2 (RS): K2, p1, *k1tbl, p2* to last 4 sts, k1tbl, p1, k2.
Row 3 (WS): P2, k1, p1, *k2, p1* to last 3 sts, k1, p2.

Row 4 (make buttonhole): K2, yo, k2tog, p2, *k1tbl, p2* to last 4 sts, k1tbl, p1, k2.
Row 5: As Row 3.
Row 6: As Row 2.
BO loosely in 1 x 2 twisted rib patt.

Sizes 2 yr, 4 yr, 6 yr, 8 yr and 10 yr only
Change to US 8 / 4 mm DPNS and work as folls:
Rnd 1: *K1tbl, p2* to end.
Work in 1 x 2 twisted rib patt as est until work measures – (–, 1, 1.5) (1.5, 1.5, 1.5)" / – (–, 2.5, 4) (4, 4, 4) cm.
BO loosely in 1 x 2 twisted rib patt.

FINISHING

Use 3-Needle Bind-Off or Grafting to join underarm sts. Weave in ends, closing any gaps that remain at the underarms. For sizes 6–12 mos and 12–18 mos, sew button to correspond to buttonhole on neckband. Block to measurements.

CHART A

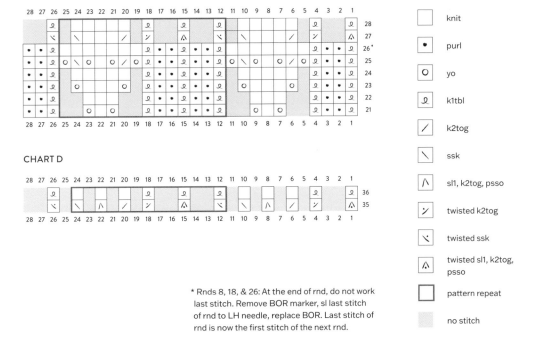

CHART B

CHART C

CHART D

knit

• purl

O yo

Ω k1tbl

∕ k2tog

∖ ssk

⋀ sl1, k2tog, psso

⋋ twisted k2tog

⋌ twisted ssk

⋀ twisted sl1, k2tog, psso

pattern repeat

no stitch

* Rnds 8, 18, & 26: At the end of rnd, do not work last stitch. Remove BOR marker, sl last stitch of rnd to LH needle, replace BOR. Last stitch of rnd is now the first stitch of the next rnd.

dancer in
the daylight

ARVI

My son, like many babies, was born without hair.
A warm hat is a winter necessity for any child — that
is why my book would not be complete without a cold
weather favourite like Arvi, named after this cute
little wearer.

Yarn B: 1 (1, 1) skein of Leona by Emilia & Philomene (72% mohair, 28% murrant silk, 459 yds / 420 m – 50 g), colourway Perugia
Or 70 (80, 95) yds / 64 (73, 86) m of lace-weight yarn

Both yarns are held together throughout pattern.

Needles: US 4 / 3.5 mm 16" / 40 cm circular needles (optional) and a set of DPNs. US 6 / 4 mm 16" / 40 cm circular needles (optional) and a set of DPNs

Notions: Stitch markers, tapestry needle

GAUGE

22 sts x 30 rows to 4" / 10 cm on US 6 / 4 mm needles in St St with yarns A and B held together, after blocking

22 sts x 32 rows to 4" / 10 cm on US 6 / 4 mm needles in Broken Garter Ridge St with yarns A and B held together, after blocking

STITCH PATTERN

BROKEN GARTER RIDGE PATT (WORKED IN THE RND, MULTIPLE OF 4 STS)
Rnds 1 and 2: K1, p2, *k2, p2* to last st, k1.
Rnd 3: K.
Rnd 4: P.
Rep rnds 1–4 for patt.

SIZES

1–2 yrs (4–6 yrs, 8–10 yrs)
Recommended ease: For a snug with approx. 1–2" / 2.5–5 cm of negative ease

FINISHED MEASUREMENTS

Circumference: 16 (18, 20)" / 40.5 (45.5, 51) cm
Length (with cuff folded over): 8 (8.5, 9)" / 20.5 (21.5, 23) cm

MATERIALS

Yarn:
Yarn A: 1 (1, 1) skein of Mr Bouthilette by Emilia & Philomene (85% blue faced leicester wool, 15% nylon, 438 yds / 400 m – 100 g), colourway Perugia
Or 70 (80, 95) yds / 64 (73, 86) m of fingering-weight yarn

NOTES

Hat instructions are written for a set of DPNs. However, an alternate method of working small circumferences, such as Magic-Loop Method or short circular needles, can be used. Change to DPNs or your preferred method for small circumference knitting in the round when necessary when you decrease for the crown.

INSTRUCTIONS

The hat is worked from the brim up to the crown in the round. It has a wide, foldable brim for extra warmth and comfort. A Broken Garter Ridge Pattern adds contrast and interest.

BRIM

Using US 4 / 3.5 mm set of DPNs and one strand each of A and B held together throughout, CO 88 (100, 112) sts using the Long-Tail CO Method, or your preferred method. Join in the rnd making sure sts are not twisted. PM for BOR.

Rnd 1: *K1, p1* to end.
Cont in 1 x 1 rib as est until work measures 6" / 15 cm from CO edge or to desired length.

Change to US 6 / 4 mm set of DPNs.

CROWN

Rep rnds 1–4 for Broken Garter Ridge Patt until work measures 11 (11.5, 12)" / 28 (29, 30.5) cm from CO edge or to desired length, ending with a rnd 2 of patt.

Next Rnd: *K22 (25, 28), PM*, rep *–* 2 more times, k to end. (3 new m's placed)

SHAPE CROWN

Rnd 1 (Dec): K2tog, *patt as est to 2 sts bef next m, ssk, SM, k2tog*, rep *–* 2 more times, patt as est to 2 sts bef BOR m, ssk. (8 sts dec'd)
Rnd 2: K1, *patt as est to 1 st bef next m, k1, SM, k1*, rep *–* 2 more times, patt as est to 1 st bef BOR m, k1.
Cont in this manner, that is, working dec rnd every other rnd 8 (8, 9) more times, then every rnd 1 (2, 3) times. (8 sts rem)

FINISHING

Break yarn, leaving a 8" / 20 cm long tail and thread onto a tapestry needle. Draw through rem sts and pull tight to close top of hat. Fasten off, weave in ends and block to measurements.

Galicia is a region of Spain known for its diverse landscapes of both green forests and glorious mountain ranges. This cardigan was designed to be warm enough for a trip to the snowy peaks, while the delicate flower pattern is an ode to the enchanting woods.

GALICIA

0–3 mos (3–6 mos, 6–12 mos, 12–18 mos, 2 yr) (4 yr, 6 yr, 8 yr, 10 yr)
Recommended ease: 2" / 5 cm of positive ease
Shown in size 4 yr on Amanda (height 38" / 97 cm)

FINISHED MEASUREMENTS

Chest Circumference: 15.25 (17, 19.25, 21, 23.25) (25, 27.25, 29, 31.25)" / 38 (43, 48, 53, 58) (63, 68, 73, 78) cm
Yoke Depth (front): 3.5 (4, 4.5, 5, 5) (5.5, 6.25, 6.5, 7)" / 9 (10, 11, 13, 13) (14, 15, 16, 17) cm
Body Length to Underarm (at front): 3.25 (3.75, 4.5, 4.75, 5.75) (6.25, 7.5, 8.5, 9)" / 8 (9, 11, 12, 14) (16, 19, 21, 23) cm
Upper Arm Circumference: 6.5 (7, 8, 8.25, 9) (9.75, 10.5, 11, 11.25)" / 16 (17, 20, 21, 23) (25, 26, 27, 28) cm
Sleeve Length to Underarm: 5.75 (6, 7, 8, 8.5) (10, 11.5, 13, 14)" / 15 (15, 18, 20, 21) (25, 29, 33, 35.5) cm

MATERIALS

Yarn: 2 (3, 4, 4, 5) (5, 7, 8, 9) skeins of 2 Ply Jumper Weight by Jamieson & Smith (100% Shetland wool, 125 yds / 115 m – 25 g), colourway FC50
Or 238 (292, 378, 437, 536) (625, 788, 919, 1042) yds / 217 (267, 345, 399, 490) (571, 720, 840, 952) m of fingering-weight yarn

Fabric: 0.3 yds / 0.25 m of cotton fabric (approx 45" / 115 cm wide)

Needles: US 5 /3.75 mm 16" / 40 cm circular needles (optional), 24" / 60 cm and a set of DPNs. US 6 / 4 mm 16" / 40 cm circular needles (optional), 24" / 60 cm and a set of DPNs

Notions: Stitch markers, stitch holders or waste yarn, tapestry needle, 5 (5, 6, 6, 7) (7, 7, 7, 7) small buttons, embroidery needle, hand sewing needle, all purpose sewing thread, small scissor

GAUGE

22 sts x 30 rows to 4" / 10 cm on US 6 / 4 mm needles in St St, after blocking

NOTES

Sleeve instructions are written for DPNs. However, an alternate method of working small circumferences, such as Magic-Loop Method or short circular needles, can be used for the larger sizes. As the yoke increases, change to longer circular needles when necessary.

INSTRUCTIONS

The cardigan is knit from the top down with a circular yoke. A small section of short rows is worked at the back of the neck and above the hem for a more comfortable fit. Embroidery is worked from a diagram. Linings for pockets, front bands and neck are drafted, cut from fabric and sewn in place by hand.

BODY

NECKBAND
With US 5 / 3.75 mm 24" / 60 circular needles, CO 55 (61, 67, 75, 79) (87, 91, 95, 101) sts using the Long-Tail CO Method, or your preferred method. You will continue to work flat.

Row 1: *K1, p1* to last st, k1.
Row 2: P1, *k1, p1* to end.
Rep rows 1 and 2, 1 (1, 1, 1, 1) (1, 2, 2, 2) more time(s).
Rep row 1 once more.

Change to US 6 / 4 mm 24" / 60 circular needles and work as foll:
Next Row (WS): K.

Sizes 0–3 mos, 3–6 mos, 6–12 mos, 12–18 mos, 2 yr, 4 yr and 8 yr only
Adjustment Row: K10 (9, 9, 5, 9) (3, –, 8, –), *m1l, k9 (7, 6, 5, 4) (6, –, 3, –)* to last 0 (3, 4, 0, 6) (0, –, 6, –) st(s), k0 (3, 4, 0, 6) (0, –, 6, –). [60 (68, 76, 89, 95) (101, –, 122, –) sts]

Sizes 6 yr and 10 yr only
Adjustment Row: K– (–, –, –, –) (–, 7, –, 2), *m1l, k3, m1l, k4* to last – (–, –, –, –) (–, 7, –, 1) st(s), m1l, k– (–, –, –, –) (–, 7, –, 1). [– (–, –, –, –) (–, 114, –, 130) sts]

All sizes resume
WORK BACK NECK SHAPING
Short Row 1 (WS): P48 (54, 58, 66, 73) (80, 87, 97, 105), turn.
Short Row 2 (RS): MDS, k35 (39, 39, 42, 50) (58, 59, 71, 79), turn.
Short Row 3 (WS): MDS, p to 4 (4, 4, 4, 4) (5, 5, 5, 6) sts bef the DS, turn.
Short Row 4 (RS): MDS, k to 4 (4, 4, 4, 4) (5, 5, 5, 6) sts bef the DS, turn.
Rep short rows 3 and 4, 1 (1, 1, 1, 2) (2, 2, 3, 3) more time(s).

Next Row (WS): MDS, p to end of row, working the DSs as one (like a p2tog). [60 (68, 76, 89, 95) (101, 114, 122, 130) sts]

Sizes 0–3 mos, 3–6 mos and 6–12 mos only
Inc Row: K2, *m1l, k2* to end, and at same time, work the rem DSs as one (like a k2tog). [89 (101, 113, –, –) (–, –, –, –) sts]
Next Row: P.
Work 6 (6, 8, –, –) (–, –, –, –) rows in St St.
Inc Row: K2, *m1l, k3* to end. [118 (134, 150, –, –) (–, –, –, –) sts]
Next Row: P.
Work 6 (6, 8, –, –) (–, –, –, –) rows in St St.
Inc Row: K3, *m1l, k4* to last 3 sts, m1l, k3. [147 (167, 187, –, –) (–, –, –, –) sts]
Next Row: P.
Work 4 (8, 8, –, –) (–, –, –, –) rows in St St.

Sizes 12–18 mos, 2 yr and 4 yr only
Inc Row: K2, *m1l, k3* to end, and at same time, work the rem DSs as one (like a k2tog). [– (–, –, 118, 126) (134, –, –, –) sts]
Next Row: P.
Work – (–, –, 6, 6) (8, –, –, –) rows in St St.
Inc Row: K3, *m1l, k4* to last 3 sts, m1l, k3. [– (–, –, 147, 157) (167, –, –, –) sts]
Next Row: P.
Work – (–, –, 6, 6) (8, –, –, –) rows in St St.
Inc Row: K3, *m1l, k5* to last 4 sts, m1l, k4. [– (–, –, 176, 188) (200, –, –, –) sts]
Next Row: P.
Work – (–, –, 6, 6) (8, –, –, –) rows in St St.
Inc Row: K4, *m1l, k6* to last 4 sts, m1l, k4. [– (–, –, 205, 219) (233, –, –, –) sts]

Next Row: P.
Work – (–, –, 8, 8) (6, –, –, –) rows in St St.

Sizes 6 yr, 8 yr and 10 yr only
Inc Row: K3, *m1l, k4* to last 3 sts, m1l, k3, and at same time, work the rem DSs as one (like a k2tog). [– (–, –, –, –) (–, 142, 152, 162) sts]
Next Row: P.
Work – (–, –, –, –) (–, 6, 6, 8) rows in St St.
Inc Row: K3, *m1l, k5* to last 4 sts, m1l, k4. [– (–, –, –, –) (–, 170, 182, 194) sts]
Next Row: P.
Work – (–, –, –, –) (–, 6, 6, 8) rows in St St.
Inc Row: K4, *m1l, k6* to last 4 sts, m1l, k4. – (–, –, –, –) (–, 198, 212, 226) sts]
Next Row: P.
Work – (–, –, –, –) (–, 6, 6, 8) rows St St.
Inc Row: K4, *m1l, k7* to last 5 sts, m1l, k5. [– (–, –, –, –) (–, 226, 242, 258) sts]
Next Row: P.
Work – (–, –, –, –) (–, 6, 6, 8) rows in St St.
Inc Row: K5, *m1l, k8* to last 5 sts, m1l, k5. [– (–, –, –, –) (–, 254, 272, 290) sts]
Next Row: P.
Work – (–, –, –, –) (–, 8, 10, 6) rows in St St.

All sizes resume
Adjustment Row: K, dec 3 (9, 9, 13, 11) (7, 12, 16, 18) sts evenly spaced around. [144 (158, 178, 192, 208) (226, 242, 256, 272) sts]
P 1 row.

DIVIDE FOR BODY
Next Row (RS): K19 (22, 24, 27, 29) (32, 34, 37, 40), pl next 33 (35, 40, 42, 45) (49, 52, 54, 56) sts from left sleeve on to waste yarn, using Backwards Loop Method, CO 3 (3, 4, 4, 5) (5, 6, 6, 6) sts for left underarm, k across next 40 (44, 50, 54, 60) (64, 70, 74, 80) sts for back, pl next 33 (35, 40, 42, 45) (49, 52, 54, 56) sts from right sleeve on to waste yarn, using Backwards Loop Method, CO 3 (3, 4, 4, 5) (5, 6, 6, 6) sts for right underarm, k to end. [84 (94, 106, 116, 128) (138, 150, 160, 172) sts]
Next Row: P21 (23, 26, 29, 32) (34, 37, 40, 43), PM for side, p42 (48, 54, 58, 64) (70, 76, 80, 86), PM for side, p to end.

Work in St St until body measures approx. 1 (1, 1.25, 1.25, 1.75) (2.75, 3, 3.5, 4)" / 3 (3, 3, 3, 4) (7, 8, 9, 10) cm from underarm ending with a p row.

POCKET OPENINGS

Beg opening for pockets as foll:

Next Row: K to first m, RM, turn. Leave rem 63 (71, 80, 87, 96) (104, 113, 120, 129) sts on waste yarn or st holder.

Working back and forth on the 21 (23, 26, 29, 32) (34, 37, 40, 43) sts, work 10 (10, 10, 18, 180 (18, 22, 22, 26) rows in St St. You will have ended on a k row. Leave these sts on waste yarn or st holder.

With RS of work facing, join yarn to next 63 (71, 80, 87, 96) (104, 113, 120, 129) sts, k to m, RM, turn. Leave rem 21 (23, 26, 29, 32) (34, 37, 40, 43) sts on waste yarn or st holder.

Working back and forth on the 42 (48, 54, 58, 64) (70, 76, 80, 86) back sts, work 10 (10, 10, 18, 18) (18, 22, 22, 26) rows in St St. You will have ended on a k row. Leave these sts on waste yarn or st holder.

With RS of work facing, join yarn to rem 21 (23, 26, 29, 32) (34, 37, 40, 43) sts, work 11 (11, 11, 19, 19) (19, 23, 23, 27) rows in St St. You will have ended on a k row.

Next Row: P21 (23, 26, 29, 32) (34, 37, 40, 43), PM for side, p across 42 (48, 54, 58, 64) (70, 76, 80, 86) sts from waste yarn for back, PM for side, p across rem 21 (23, 26, 29, 32) (34, 37, 40, 43) sts from waste yarn for left front. [84 (94, 106, 116, 128) (138, 150, 160, 172) sts]

If necessary, cont in St St until body measures approx. 2.25 (2.75, 3.5, 3.75, 4.75) (5.25, 6, 7, 7.5)" / 6 (7, 9, 9, 12) (13, 15, 18, 19) cm from underarm or 0.75 (0.75, 0.75, 0.75, 0.75) (0.75, 1, 1, 1)" / 2 (2, 2, 2, 2) (2, 3, 3, 3) cm less than desired length to start of lower hem ending with a WS row.

WORK LOWER BACK SHAPING

Short Row 1 (RS): K to first m, SM, k to next m, SM, k3 (3, 3, 3, 3) (5, 5, 5, 6), turn.
Short Row 2 (WS): MDS, p to first m, SM, p to next m, SM, p3 (3, 3, 3, 3) (5, 5, 5, 6), turn.
Short Row 3 (RS): MDS, slipping m as needed, k to 4 (4, 4, 4, 4) (7, 7, 7, 8) sts bef the DS, turn.
Short Row 4 (WS): MDS, p to 4 (4, 4, 4, 4) (7, 7, 7, 8) sts bef the DS, turn.
Rep short rows 3 and 4, 0 (0, 0, 0, 1) (1, 1, 2, 2) more time(s).

Next Row (RS): MDS, k to end, working the DSs as one (like a k2tog). [84 (94, 106, 116, 128) (138, 150, 160, 172) sts]
Next Row (WS): K, inc 1 st at centre back using an m1l, and at same time, work the rem DSs as one (like a k2tog). [85 (95, 107, 117, 129) (139, 151, 161, 173) sts]

LOWER HEM

With US 5 / 3.75 mm 24" / 60 cm circular needles and work as foll:
Row 1: *K1, p1* to last st, k1.
Row 2: P1, *k1, p1* to end.
Rep rows 1 and 2, 2 (2, 2, 2, 2) (2, 3, 3, 3) more times.
BO evenly in rib patt.

SLEEVES

Pl 33 (35, 40, 42, 45) (49, 52, 54, 56) sts on waste yarn for right sleeve onto US 6 / 4 mm set of DPNs or preferred style for working small circumferences, and beg at centre of underarm, pick up and k 1 (1, 2, 2, 2) (2, 3, 3, 3) st(s) along underarm CO sts, k34 (34, 38, 42, 46) (50, 54, 54, 58) sts from sleeve, and then pick up and k 2 (2, 2, 2, 3) (3, 3, 3, 3) sts along underarm CO to centre. PM for BOR. [36 (38, 44, 46, 50) (54, 58, 60, 62) sts]

Work 7 (5, 4, 8, 7) (9, 6, 9, 9) rnds in St St.
Dec Rnd: K1, ssk, k to last 3 sts, k2tog, k1. (2 sts dec'd)
Rep dec rnd every 10th (8th, 8th, 8th, 8th) (8th, 8th, 8th, 8th) rnd 2 (3, 4, 3, 2) (4, 3, 7, 8) more times, then every 0 (0, 0, 6th, 6th) (6th, 6th, 6th, 6th) rnd 0 (0, 0, 2, 4) (3, 6, 2, 2) more time(s). [30 (30, 34, 34, 36) (38, 38, 40, 40) sts]

If necessary, work even in St St in the rnd until sleeve measures 5 (5.25, 6.25, 7.25, 7.75) (9.25, 10.5, 12, 13)" / 13 (13, 16, 18, 19) (23, 26, 30, 33) cm or 0.75 (0.75, 0.75, 0.75, 0.75) (0.75, 1, 1, 1)" / 2 (2, 2, 2, 2) (2, 3, 3, 3) cm less than desired length to start of sleeve cuff.

Next Rnd: P.

SLEEVE CUFF

With US 5 / 3.75 mm set of DPNs, work as foll:
Rnd 1: *K1, p1* to end.
Cont in est 1 x 1 rib for 5 (5, 5, 5, 5) (5, 7, 7, 7) more rnds.
BO evenly in 1 x 1 rib patt.

Work second sleeve as first.

want to see
my secret?

BUTTON BANDS

LEFT FRONT BUTTON BAND

With RS facing and using US 5 / 3.75 mm 24" / 60 cm circular needles, pick up and k 42 (50, 52, 58, 66) (70, 74, 80, 86) sts evenly down left front edge (approx. 3 sts for every 4 rows).

Row 1: *K1, p1* to end.
Cont in est 1 x 1 rib for 4 (4, 4, 4, 4) (4, 6, 6, 6) more rows.
BO evenly in 1 x 1 rib patt.

RIGHT FRONT BUTTONHOLE BAND

Sizes 0–3 mos, 3–6 mos, 6–12 mos, 12–18 mos, 2 yr and 4 yr only
With RS facing and using US 5 / 3.75 mm 24" / 60 cm circular needles, pick up and k sts as bef, evenly up right front edge. [42 (50, 52, 58, 66) (70, –, –, –) sts]
Row 1: *K1, p1* to end.
Rep row 1 once more.
Next Row (make buttonholes): K1, p1, *k2tog, yo, (k1, p1) 3 (4, 3, 4, 4) (4, –, –, –) times*, rep *–* 3 (3, 4, 4, 5) (5, –, –, –) more times, k2tog, yo, *k1, p1* 3 (3, 4, 2, 1) (3, –, –, –) time(s).
Rep row 1, 2 more times.
BO evenly in 1 x 1 rib patt.

Sizes 6 yr, 8 yr and 10 yr only
With RS facing and using US 5 / 3.75 mm 24" / 60 cm circular needles, pick up and k sts as bef, evenly up right front edge. [– (–, –, –, –) (–, 74, 80, 86) sts]
Row 1: *K1, p1* to end.
Rep row 1, 2 more times.

Next Row (make buttonholes): *K1, p1* – (–, –, –, –) (–, 5, 2, 5) times, *k2tog, yo, (k1, p1) – (–, –, –, –) (–, 4, 5, 5) times*, rep *–* – (–, –, –, –) (–, 5, 5, 5) more times, k2tog, yo, k1, p1.
Rep row 1, 3 more times.
BO evenly in 1 x 1 rib patt.

FINISHING

Weave in ends, closing any gaps that remain at the underarms. Using embroidery needle and yarn, complete the flower embroidery around the yoke using the diagram as your guide and scattering the flowers around the yoke to your desire. Sew buttons

to correspond to buttonholes on left front button band after fabric band is sewn on (instructions below). Block to measurements.

POCKET LINING (MAKE 2 FROM FABRIC)

Cut a semi circle from a piece of paper that is approx. 3 (3, 3, 5.5, 5.5) (5.5, 6.5, 6.5, 7.5)" / 8 (8, 8, 14, 14) (14, 16, 16, 19) cm in diameter by 2 (2, 2, 2.5, 2.5) (2.5, 3, 3, 3.5)" / 5 (5, 5, 6, 6) (6, 8, 8, 9) cm in depth (see diagram). Using the semi circle as your pattern piece, cut 2 pocket linings from your fabric.

Fold the straight edge to the inside for a 0.25" / 0.75 cm selvedge. Press with an iron and slip stitch the selvedge edge in place. Fold the pocket lining in half, RS tog, creating a "wedge" shape. Using a 0.25" / 0.75 cm seam allowance, hand stitch along the rounded edge, creating a little pocket. Turn the pocket to the right side. Insert the pocket into the pocket opening of the cardigan with the rounded edge facing downwards. Sew the pocket lining in place around the pocket opening with edges slightly peeking out to the front of the cardigan.

Make second pocket lining as the first.

NECKBAND
Cut a strip of fabric that is approx. 4" / 10 cm wide and fits evenly along neck band plus an extra 0.5" / 1.25 cm for turning in the selvedge edges. With wrong sides together, fold the strip in half lengthwise (now approx. 2" / 5.25 cm wide). Press with an iron, creating a centre fold. Open up the fold and fold in each long raw edge to the centre fold line with wrong sides together. Press with an iron. Fold in half again on the centre fold line, creating a strip that is now approx. 1" / 2.5 cm wide. Press with an iron.

Fold each short end of the strip to the inside for a 0.25" / 0.75 cm selvedge. Pin neatly along the inside of the neck band. Slip stitch in place.

FRONT BANDS
Create 2 strips for front bands in same manner as neckbands. Turning in the selvedge edges, pin one strip neatly along the button band and slip stitch in place.

Turning in the selvedge edges, pin the other strip neatly along the buttonhole band. Mark each buttonhole. With the tip of a small scissor, carefully cut a tiny slit to match each buttonhole. Slip stitch the strip in place.

SLEEVE CUFFS
Create 2 strips for sleeve cuffs in same manner as neckbands. Pin each strip neatly along the inside of a sleeve cuff. Slip stitch in place.

FLOWER EMBROIDERY FOR YOKE

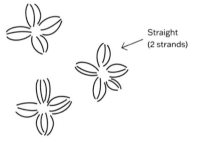

Straight
(2 strands)

POCKET LINING

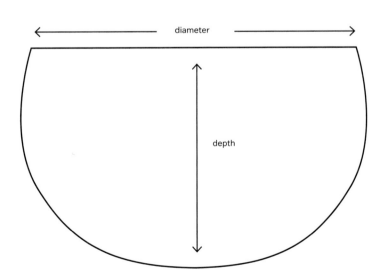

diameter

depth

ANGEL
TRUMPET

My elementary school in El Salvador was surrounded by angel
trumpets, a common flower whose appearance is very true
to its name. This sweater, with the yoke and balloon sleeves,
reminds me of this beautiful nightshade.

SIZES

0–3 mos (3–6 mos, 6–12 mos, 12–18 mos, 2 yr) (4 yr, 6 yr, 8 yr, 10 yr)
Recommended ease: 2" / 5 cm of positive ease at chest
Shown in size 4 yr on Ilana (height 38" / 97 cm)

FINISHED MEASUREMENTS

Chest Circumference: 17.25 (19.25, 21.25, 23.25, 25.25) (27.25, 29.25, 31.25, 33.25)" / 43 (48, 53, 58, 63) (68, 73, 78, 83) cm
Yoke Depth (front): 4 (4, 4.5, 5, 5) (5.5, 6, 6.5, 7)" / 10 (10, 11.5, 12.75, 12.75) (14, 15.25, 16.5, 17.75)
Body Length to Underarm (front): 4 (4.5, 5, 5.5, 6) (7.5, 9, 10, 11)" / 10 (11, 13, 14, 15) (19, 23, 25, 28) cm
Upper Arm Circumference: 6.5 (7, 7.5, 7.75, 8.25) (9.5, 10.25, 10.5, 10.75)" / 17 (18, 19, 20, 21) (24, 26, 26, 27) cm
Sleeve Length to Underarm: 3.75 (4, 5, 6, 6) (7.5, 9, 10.5, 11.5)" / 9 (10, 13, 15, 15) (19, 23, 26, 29) cm

MATERIALS

Yarn: 1 (2, 2, 2, 2) (3, 4, 4, 5) skein(s) of Daylights by Harrisville (Woolen-spun American Cormo & wool, 250 yds / 229 m – 100 g), colourway Lint

Or 1 (2, 2, 2, 2) (3, 4, 4, 5) skein(s) of Dovestone by Baa Ram Ewe (50% bluefaced leicester, 25% masham/massam, 25% wensleydale, 252 yds / 223 m – 100 g), colourway Aire (7)

Or 238 (278, 349, 425, 472) (612, 760, 895, 1027) yds / 217 (254, 319, 388, 431) (559, 694, 818, 939) m of DK-weight yarn

Needles: US 5 / 3.75 mm 16" / 40 cm circular needles (optional for sizes 2–10 yrs), 24" / 60 cm and a set of DPNs. US 6 / 4 mm 16" / 40 cm circular needles (optional for 2–10 yrs), 24" / 60 cm and a set of DPNs

Notions: Stitch marker, waste yarn or stitch holders, tapestry needle, 1 button (baby sizes only)

GAUGE

20 sts x 30 rows to 4" / 10 cm on US 6 / 4 mm needles in St St, after blocking

SPECIAL ABBREVIATIONS

CDD: Central double decrease: Slip 2 sts together as if to knit to your right-hand needle. Knit the next stitch. Pass the slipped stitches over the knit stitch. (2 sts dec'd)

NOTES

Sleeve instructions are written for DPNs. However, an alternate method of working small circumferences, such as Magic-Loop Method or short circular needles, can be used.

As the yoke decreases, change to shorter circular needles when necessary. Four smallest sizes have a button closure at back neck and will require a button.

The yoke is read from a chart. The chart is read from bottom to top and from right to left when knitting in the rnd.

INSTRUCTIONS

The pullover is worked from the bottom up with a circular yoke. The sleeves are worked separately in the round to the base of the yoke, then joined. A section of short rows is worked at the bottom of the back yoke and at the back neck for a more comfortable fit.

SLEEVES

Using US 5 / 3.75 mm set of DPNs, CO 28 (30, 30, 32, 32) (34, 34, 36, 38) sts using the Long-Tail CO Method, or your preferred method. Join in the rnd making sure sts are not twisted. PM for BOR.

Rnd 1: *K1, p1* to end.
Cont in est 1 x 1 rib for 5 more rnds.

Change to US 6 / 4 mm set of DPNs or preferred needles for small circumference knitting, and work as foll:

Sizes 0–3 mos, 3–6 mos, 6–12 mos, 12–18 mos, 2 yr and 4 yr only
Inc Rnd: K, inc 5 (5, 7, 7, 9) (13, –, –, –) sts evenly around, using an m1l. [33 (35, 37, 39, 41) (47, –, –, –) sts]

Sizes 6 yr, 8 yr and 10 yr only
Inc Rnd: K- (-, -, -, -) (-, 0, 2, 3), *m1l, k2* to last- (-, -, -, -) (-, 0, 0, 1) st, k- (-, -, -, -) (-, 0, 0, 1). [- (-, -, -, -) (-, 51, 53, 55) sts]

All sizes resume
Work in St St in the rnd until sleeve measures 3.75 (4, 5, 6, 6) (7.5, 9, 10.5, 11.5)" / 9 (10, 13, 15, 15) (19, 23, 26, 29) cm from CO edge, or desired length to underarm.

Next Rnd: K, ending 2 (2, 3, 3, 3) (3, 4, 4, 4) sts bef BOR m.

Pl next 3 (3, 5, 5, 5) (5, 7, 7, 7) sts on waste yarn or st holder for underarm, removing m when come to it. Break yarn. [30 (32, 32, 34, 36) (42, 44, 46, 48) sts] Set aside first sleeve, pl rem 30 (32, 32, 34, 36) (42, 44, 46, 48) sts on waste yarn or spare needle. Work second sleeve as first.

BODY

Using US 5 / 3.75 mm 16" / 40 cm circular needles (or longer for child sizes), CO 86 (96, 106, 116, 126) (136, 146, 156, 166) sts using the Long-Tail CO Method, or your preferred method. Join in the rnd making sure sts are not twisted. PM for BOR.

Rnd 1: *K1, p1* to end.
Cont in est 1 x 1 rib for 5 more rnds.

Change to US 6 / 4 mm 16" / 40 cm circular needles (or longer for child sizes).
Work in St St in the rnd until work measures 4 (4.5, 5, 5.5, 6) (7.5, 9, 10, 11)" / 10 (11.5, 12.75, 14, 15.25) (19, 23, 25.5, 28) cm from CO edge or desired length to underarm.

JOIN FOR YOKE

Next Rnd: Removing BOR m, k across 20 (23, 24, 27, 29) (32, 33, 36, 38) sts for left back. Pl next 3 (3, 5, 5, 5) (5, 7, 7, 7) sts on waste yarn for left underarm. Transfer sts from first sleeve on to LHN of body, and k30 (32, 32, 34, 36) (42, 44, 46, 48) sts for left sleeve. K across 40 (44, 48, 52, 58) (62, 66, 70, 76) sts for front, pl next 3 (3, 5, 5, 5) (5, 7, 7, 7) sts on waste yarn for right underarm. Transfer sts from second sleeve on to LHN of body and k30 (32, 32, 34, 36) (42, 44, 46, 48) sts for right sleeve,

then k across rem 20 (23, 24, 27, 29) (32, 33, 36, 38) sts for right back. PM for new BOR (centre back). [140 (154, 160, 174, 188) (210, 220, 234, 248) sts]
Adjustment Rnd: K6 (4, 2, 6, 3) (8, 1, 12, 11), *k2tog, k7 (7, 9, 8, 8) (6, 7, 6, 6)* to last 8 (6, 4, 8, 5) (10, 3, 14, 13) sts, k2tog, k to BOR. [125 (137, 145, 157, 169) (185, 195, 207, 219) sts]
K 0 (0, 0, 0, 0) (1, 1, 2, 2) rnd(s).

WORK BACK YOKE SHORT ROWS
Short Row 1 (RS): K31 (35, 36, 40, 42) (47, 49, 52, 55), turn.
Short Row 2 (WS): MDS, p to BOR m, SM, p31 (35, 36, 40, 42) (47, 49, 52, 55), turn.
Short Row 3 (RS): MDS, slipping BOR m, k to 2 (2, 3, 3, 3) (5, 5, 5, 5) sts bef the DS, turn.
Short Row 4 (WS): MDS, slipping BOR m, p to 2 (2, 3, 3, 3) (5, 5, 5, 5) sts bef the DS, turn.
Rep short rows 3 and 4, 0 (0, 1, 1, 1) (2, 2, 2, 2) more time(s).

Next Short Row (RS): MDS, k to 3 (3, 5, 5, 5) (7, 7, 7, 7) sts bef the DS, turn.
Next Short Row (WS): MDS, p to 3 (3, 5, 5, 5) (7, 7, 7, 7) sts bef the DS, turn.
Next Row (RS): MDS, k to BOR m.
Next Rnd: K to end, working the DSs as one (like a k2tog). [125 (137, 145, 157, 169) (185, 195, 207, 219) sts]
K 0 (0, 0, 0, 0) (1, 5, 8, 11) rnds.
Adjustment Rnd: K6 (4, 1, 6, 3) (8, 0, 12, 11), *k2tog, k6 (6, 8, 7, 7) (5, 6, 5, 5)* to last 7 (5, 4, 7, 4) (9, 3, 13, 12) sts, k2tog, k5 (3, 2, 5, 2) (7, 1, 11, 10). [110 (120, 130, 140, 150) (160, 170, 180, 190) sts]
K 0 (0, 1, 0, 0) (1, 1, 1, 1) rnd.

BEGIN YOKE PATTERN
Change to 16" / 40 cm circular needles or set of DPNs as necessary.

Beg working yoke patt from the Chart, working the 10-st rep 11 (12, 13, 14, 15) (16, 17, 18, 19) times around, and working decs where indicated until 28 (28, 28, 33, 33) (33, 33, 33, 33) rnds of chart are complete. [88 (96, 104, 70, 75) (80, 85, 90, 95) sts]

Size 0–3 mos only
Adjustment Rnd: K6, *k2tog, k1* to last 7 sts, k2tog, k5. (62 sts)

Size 6–12 mos only
Adjustment Rnd: K, dec 2 sts evenly spaced around. (102 sts)

Size 3–6 mos and 6–12 mos only
Adjustment Rnd: *K1, k2tog* evenly spaced around. [– (64, 68, –, –) (–, –, –, –) sts]

Sizes 12–18 mos, 2 yr, 4 yr, 6 yr, 8 yr and 10 yr only
Next Rnd: *K3, p2* to end.
Rep last rnd once more.

All sizes resume
WORK BACK YOKE SHORT ROWS
Short Row 1 (RS): Work in patt as est over next 24 (25, 26, 27, 29) (31, 32, 35, 37) sts, turn.
Short Row 2 (WS): MDS, bring yarn to back if knitting next st or bring yarn to front if purling next st, work patt as est to BOR m, SM, work patt as est over next 24 (25, 26, 27, 29) (31, 32, 35, 37) sts, turn.
Short Row 3 (RS): MDS, bring yarn to back if knitting next st or bring yarn to front if purling next st, slipping BOR m, work patt as est to 2 (2, 2, 2, 3) (3, 3, 3, 3) sts bef the DS, turn.
Short Row 4 (WS): MDS, bring yarn to back if knitting next st or bring yarn to front if purling next st, slipping BOR m, work patt as est to 2 (2, 2, 2, 3) (3, 3, 3, 3) sts bef the DS, turn.
Rep short rows 3 and 4, 0 (0, 0, 0, 1) (1, 1, 1, 1) more time.

Sizes 0–3 mos, 3–6 mos, 6–12 mos and 12–18 mos only
With US 5 / 3.75 mm 16" / 40 cm circular needles, begin working back and forth as foll:
Row 1: K to BOR m. Turn work so that WS is facing, k to end working the DSs as one (like a k2tog), then, using the Backward Loop Method, CO 3 sts. [65 (67, 71, 73, –) (–, –, –, –) sts]
Row 2 (RS): P.
Row 3 (WS): K to last 3 sts, yo, k2tog, k1.
Row 4 (RS): P.
BO loosely kwise.

Sizes 2 yr, 4 yr, 6 yr, 8 yr and 10 yr only
With US 5 / 3.75 mm set of DPNs or preferred needles for small circumference knitting, work as foll:
Rnd 1: P to end, working the DSs as one (like a p2tog).

Rnd 2: P.
Rep rnd 2, 2 more times.
BO loosely pwise.

FINISHING

Use 3-Needle Bind-Off or Grafting to join underarm sts. Weave in ends, closing any gaps that remain at the underarms. Sizes 0–3 mos, 3–6 mos, 6–12 mos and 12–18 mos sew button to correspond to buttonhole on neckband. Block to measurements.

WRITTEN INSTRUCTIONS FOR YOKE CHART

Rnd 1: *K6, p3, k1* to end.
Rnd 2: *K5, p5* to end.
Rnd 3: *P1, k3, p6* to end.
Rnd 4: As rnd 3.
Rnd 5: *K2tog, yo, k1, yo, ssk, p5* to end.
Rnd 6: As rnd 2.
Rnd 7: *(K1, yo) twice, k1, ssk, p3, k2tog* to end.
Rnd 8: As rnd 1.
Rnd 9: *K5, k2tog, yo, k1, yo, ssk* to end.
Rnd 10: As rnd 1.
Rnd 11: *Ssk, k3, k2tog, yo, p3, yo* to end.
Rnd 12: As rnd 2.
Rnd 13: *Yo, ssk, k1, k2tog, yo, p5* to end.
Rnd 14: As rnd 3.
Rnd 15: *P1, yo, CDD, yo, p6* to end.
Rnd 16: *P2, k1, p7* to end.
Rnd 17: As rnd 5.
Rnd 18: As rnd 2.
Rnd 19: As rnd 7.
Rnd 20: As rnd 1.
Rnd 21: As rnd 9.
Rnd 22: As rnd 1.
Rnd 23: As rnd 11.
Rnd 24: As rnd 2.
Rnd 25: As rnd 13.
Rnd 26: As rnd 3.
Rnd 27: As rnd 15.
Rnd 28: *P2, k1, p2tog, p2, p2tog, p1* to end. (2 sts dec'd in each rep)

Sizes 12–18 mos, 2 yr, 4 yr, 6 yr, 8 yr and 10 yr only
Rnd 29: *P2, k1, p5* to end.
Rnd 30: *P2tog, k1, p2tog, p3* to end. (2 sts dec'd in each rep)
Rnd 31: *P1, k1, p4* to end.
Rnd 32: *P1, k1, p1, p2tog, p1* to end, (1 st dec'd in each rep)
Rnd 33: *P1, k1, p3* to end.

Yoke chart

Symbols: (blank) = knit, • = purl, O = yo, / = k2tog, \ = ssk, Λ = CDD, ⟋ = p2tog, ▨ = no stitch

Row	10	9	8	7	6	5	4	3	2	1
33	▨	▨	▨	▨	▨	•	•	•		•
32	▨	▨	▨	▨	•	▨	⟋	•		•
31	▨	▨	▨	▨	•	•	•	•		•
30	▨	▨	•	•	•	▨	⟋		▨	⟋
29	▨	▨	•	•	•	•	•		•	•
28	•	▨	⟋	•	•	▨	⟋		•	•
27	•	•	•	•	•	•	O	Λ	O	•
26	•	•	•	•	•	•				•
25	•	•	•	•	•	O	/		\	O
24	•	•	•	•	•					
23	O	•	•	•	O	/				\
22		•	•	•						
21	\	O		O	/					
20		•	•	•						
19	/	•	•	•	\		O		O	
18	•	•	•	•	•					
17	•	•	•	•	•	\	O		O	/
16	•	•	•	•	•	•	•		•	•
15	•	•	•	•	•	•	O	Λ	O	•
14	•	•	•	•	•	•				•
13	•	•	•	•	•	O	/		\	O
12	•	•	•	•	•					
11	O	•	•	•	O	/				\
10		•	•	•						
9	\	O		O	/					
8		•	•	•						
7	/	•	•	•	\		O		O	
6	•	•	•	•	•					
5	•	•	•	•	•	\	O		O	/
4	•	•	•	•	•	•				•
3	•	•	•	•	•	•				•
2	•	•	•	•	•					
1		•	•	•						

Legend

- ☐ knit
- • purl
- O yo
- / k2tog
- \ ssk
- Λ CDD
- ⟋ p2tog
- ☐ pattern repeat
- ▨ no stitch

Note! Sizes 0–3 mos, 3–6 mos & 6–12 mos end after chart row 28.

MIDORI'S MITTENS

While these mitts keep tiny hands cosy and warm in cold weather, the adorable lilies and buzzing bees make you look forward to warmer months to come. I named the pattern after my talented friend, Midori, who embroidered all the samples for this book.

SIZES

6–18 mos (2 yr, 4 yr, 6 yr, 8 yr)

FINISHED MEASUREMENTS

Circumference: 4.75 (5.25, 5.75, 6.25, 6.75)" / 12 (13, 14, 16, 17) cm
Length: 4 (4.75, 5.25, 6, 6)" / 10 (12, 13, 15, 15) cm
Thumb Length (6–18 mos does not have a thumb):
– (1.75, 1.75, 2, 2)" / – (4, 4, 5, 5) cm

MATERIALS

Yarn: 1 (1, 2, 2, 2) skein(s) of Fingering by Tukuwool (100% wool, 213 yds / 195 m – 50 g), colourway H34 (dusty pink version), 28 (pink version) and 05 (grey version)
Or 140 (184, 222, 276, 298) yds / 128 (168, 204, 253, 273) m of fingering-weight yarn

Needles: US 1.5 / 2.5 mm set of DPNs. US 2 / 2.75 mm set of DPNs

Notions: Removable stitch markers (1 of a different colour for BOR), cable needle, waste yarn in different colour with similar gauge, tapestry needle, embroidery needle, Temaricious embroidery threads: 1 skein each of colourway Indian Matter, Logwood, Indigo and Glory-Bower

GAUGE

27 sts x 36 rnds to 4" / 10 cm on US 2 / 2.75 mm needles in St St, after blocking

SPECIAL ABBREVIATIONS

2/2 RC (2/2 Right Cross): Sl next 2 sts to CN and hold in back of work. K2, then k2 from CN.

NOTES

This pattern is written for DPNs. However, an alternate method of working small circumferences, such as Magic Loop Method, can be used. Mitten and thumb length is adjustable.

INSTRUCTIONS

The mittens are worked in the round from the cuff up. The thumb stitches are held on waste yarn and picked up from the row below and the row above the waste yarn after the body of the mittens is completed. The top of the mittens is grafted together. Finally, a touch of embroidery is added on the top of each hand.

CUFF

Using US 1.5 / 2.5 mm set of DPNs, CO 25 (30, 30, 35, 40) sts using the Long-Tail CO Method, or your preferred method. Evenly disperse sts over 4 DPNs. Join in the rnd making sure sts are not twisted. Pl a removable m for BOR.

Rnd 1: *P2, k3* to end.
Rnd 2: *P2, k1, kfb, k1* to end. [30, (36, 36, 42, 48) sts]
Rnd 3: *P2, k4* to end.
Rnd 4: *P2, 2/2 RC* to end.
Rnds 5–7: *P2, k4* to end.
Rep rnds 4–7, 2 (2, 3, 4, 4) more times.

Next Rnd: As rnd 4.

Sizes 6–18 mos and 4 yr only
Next Rnd: K1, m1l, k15 (–, 18, –, –), m1l, k to end. [32 (–, 38, –, –) sts]

Sizes 2 yr and 6 yr only
Next Rnd: K.

Size 8 yr only
Next Rnd: K1, ssk, k22, ssk, k to end. (46 sts)

All sizes resume
Change to US 2 / 2.75 mm set of DPNs.

HAND

Rnd 1: K.

Size 6–18 mos only
Note! Size 6–18 mos does not include a thumb.
Proceed to "BOTH MITTENS" on the next page.

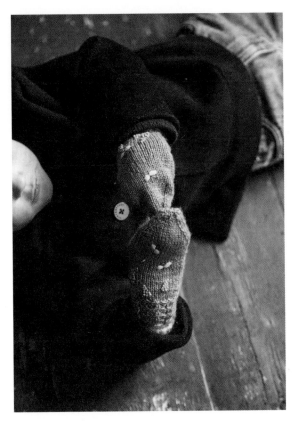

BOTH MITTENS

Cont in St St in the rnd until work measures 2.75 (3.25, 3.75, 4.25, 4)″ / 7 (8, 9.5, 11, 10) cm from top of cuff or 1.25 (1.5, 1.5, 1.75, 2)″ / 3 (4, 4, 4, 5) cm less than desired length from top of cuff to start of shaping for top of mittens.

SHAPE TOP OF MITTENS

Next Rnd: K16 (18, 19, 21, 23), pl m for side, k to end.
Dec Rnd 1: K1, ssk, k to 3 sts bef m, k2tog, k1, SM, k1, ssk, k to last 3 sts, k2tog, k1. (4 sts dec'd)
Rnd 2: K.
Rep rnds 1 and 2, 5 (6, 6, 7, 8) more times, working last rnd as foll:
Last Rnd: K dispersing sts evenly onto 2 DPNs. [8 (8, 10, 10, 10) sts, with 4 (4, 5, 5, 5) sts on each of 2 rem needles]
Break yarn leaving a long tail and Graft sts together.

MAKE THUMB

Sizes 2 yr, 4 yr, 6 yr and 8 yr only
With US 2 / 2.75 mm set of DPNs, pick up and pl – (7, 7, 8, 9) sts from the row below the waste yarn onto one DPN and – (7, 7, 8, 9) sts from the row above the waste yarn onto a second DPN. Remove waste yarn. Using main yarn and rem DPNs, pick up and k 1 st along right side of thumb opening, k across – (7, 7, 8, 9) picked up sts, pick up and k 1 st from left side of opening, k across rem – (7, 7, 8, 9) sts. [– (16, 16, 18, 20) sts]

Evenly disperse sts over 4 DPNs. Pl a removable m for BOR.
Rnd 1: K.
Cont in St St until thumb measures – (1.25, 1.25, 1.5, 1.5)″ / – (3.25, 3.25, 4, 4) cm or 0.5″ / 1.5 cm cm less than desired length of thumb.

Next Rnd: *K1, ssk, k– (2, 2, 3, 4), k2tog, k1*, rep *–* once more. (4 sts dec'd)
Next Rnd: K.
Next Rnd: *K1, ssk, k– (0, 0, 1, 2), k2tog, k1*, rep *–* once more. (4 sts dec'd)
Next Rnd: *K2tog* to end. [– (4, 4, 5, 6) sts]
Break yarn leaving a 6″ / 15 cm tail. Thread yarn onto tapestry needle and draw through rem sts. Fasten off.

Sizes 2 yr, 4 yr, 6 yr and 8 yr only
K – (17, 17, 19, 22) rnds or desired length to the base of the thumb.

LEFT MITTEN

Next Rnd: K– (27, 29, 32, 35), k– (7, 7, 8, 9) with waste yarn (for thumb), sl the – (7, 7, 8, 9) waste yarn sts back onto LHN pwise. With main yarn, k to end (including the sts on the waste yarn).

RIGHT MITTEN

Next Rnd: K– (2, 2, 2, 2), k– (7, 7, 8, 9) sts with waste yarn (for thumb), sl the – (7, 7, 8, 9) waste yarn sts back onto LHN pwise. With main yarn, k to end (including the sts on the waste yarn).

FINISHING

Weave in ends and block to measurements.
Using embroidery needle and threads, complete the
embroidery on top of each mitten using the below
diagrams as your guide.

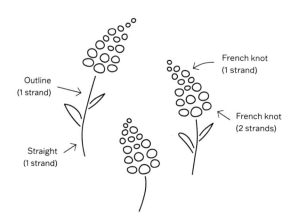

I wanted to create a symmetrical pattern of little stars in the night sky. Since the original blanket was made, others have said that they see ribbons, petals — or even pasta! No matter what people see, this design will become a lovely companion to your child.

LITTLE STAR

SIZE

One Size

FINISHED MEASUREMENTS

Length: 40" / 102 cm
Width: 36" / 91 cm

MATERIALS

Yarn: 5 skeins of Daylights by Harrisville (woolen-spun American Cormo & wool, 250 yds / 229 m – 100 g), colourway Lint
Or 1250 yds / 1143 m of DK-weight yarn

Needles: US 6 / 4 mm 32" / 80 cm circular needles

Notions: Stitch markers, cable needle, tapestry needle

GAUGE

27 sts x 27 rows to 4" / 10 cm on US 6 / 4 mm needles in 1 x 1 rib patt, after blocking

2 reps x 28 rows to 5.5 x 4" / 13.5 x 10 cm on US 6 / 4 mm needles in flower patt, after blocking

NOTES

The blanket is rectangular in shape with a flower pattern in the centre and a wide, ribbed border. Gauge is not critical but can affect the quantity of yarn used.

The central flower pattern is worked from a chart. The chart is read from bottom to top and from right to left on RS rows and from left to right on WS rows.

SPECIAL ABBREVIATIONS

2/2/2 LC (2/2/2 Left Cross): Sl next 4 sts to CN and hold in front of work. K2, sl left 2 sts from CN to LHN, then p2, k2 from CN.

INSTRUCTIONS

The blanket is worked flat with a cable pattern in the centre and a wide border in 1 x 1 Ribbing.

BOTTOM BORDER

Using US 6 / 4 mm 32" / 80 cm circular needles, CO 206 sts using the Long-Tail CO Method, or your preferred method. You will continue to work flat.

Row 1 (WS): Wyif, sl first st pwise, *p1, k1* to last st, p1.
Rep row 1, 39 more times.

CENTRE PATTERN

Row 1 (WS): Wyif, sl first st pwise, *p1, k1* 19 times, p1, PM, reading RS rows from right to left and WS rows from left to right, work row 1 of Chart over next 126 sts using chart or chart written instructions., PM, *k1, p1* to end.
Row 2 (RS): Wyif, sl first st pwise, *p1, k1* to 1 st bef m, p1, SM, work row 2 of chart over next 126 sts SM, *k1, p1* to end.

Slipping m's, cont in this manner as est, that is working appropriate rows of chart with the 1 x 1 rib patt on either side until all chart rows have been worked a total of 6 times.

Cont in patt as est until a further 27 rows of chart have been completed.

TOP BORDER

Row 1 (RS): Wyif, sl first st pwise, *p1, k1* to last st, p1.
Rep row 1, 39 more times.
BO evenly in 1 x 1 rib as est.

FINISHING

Weave in ends and block to measurements.

WRITTEN INSTRUCTIONS FOR CHART

CENTRE FLOWER PATT (WORKED FLAT OVER MULTIPLE OF 14 PLUS 28 STS)

Row 1 (WS): K1, p2, k8, *p2, k2, p2, k8* to last 17 sts, p2, k2, p2, k8, p2, k1.

Row 2 (RS): P1, k1, yo, ssk, p6, k2tog, yo, k1, p2, k1, yo, *ssk, p6, k2tog, yo, k1, p2, k1, yo* to last 12 sts, ssk, p6, k2tog, yo, k1, p1.

Row 3: K1, p3, k6, p1, *p2, k2, p3, k6, p1* to last 17 sts, p2, k2, p3, k6, p3, k1.

Row 4: P1, k2, yo, ssk, p4, k2tog, yo, k2, p2, k2, *yo, ssk, p4, k2tog, yo, k2, p2, p2* to last 11 sts, yo, ssk, p4, k2tog, yo, k2, p1.

Row 5: K1, p4, k4, p2, *p2, k2, p4, k4, p2* to last 17 sts, p2, k2, p4, k4, p4, k1.

Row 6: P1, k3, yo, ssk, p2, k2tog, yo, k3, p2, k2, *k1, yo, ssk, p2, k2tog, yo, k3, p2, k2* to last 11 sts, k1, yo, ssk, p2, k2tog, yo, k3, p1.

Row 7: K1, p5, k2, p3, *p2, k2, p5, k2, p3* to last 17 sts, p2, k2, p5, k2, p5, k1.

Row 8: P1, yo, ssk, k3, p2, k3, k2tog, yo, p2, yo, ssk, *k3, p2, k3, k2tog, yo, p2, yo, ssk* to last 11 sts, k3, p2, k3, k2tog, yo, p1.

Row 9: K2, p4, k2, k3, *p1, k4, p4, k2, p3* to last 17 sts, p1, k4, p4, k2, p4, k2.

Row 10: P2, yo, ssk, k2, p2, k2, k2tog, yo, p4, yo, *ssk, k2, p2, k2, k2tog, yo, p4, yo*, to last 12 sts, ssk, k2, p2, k2, k2tog, yo, p2.

Row 11: K3, p3, k2, p3, *k6, p3, k2, p3* to last 17 sts, k6, p3, k2, p3, k3.

Row 12: P3, yo, ssk, k1, p2, k1, k2tog, yo, p6, *yo, ssk, k1, p2, k1, k2tog, yo, p6* to last 11 sts, yo, ssk, k1, p2, k1, k2tog, yo, p3.

Row 13: K4, p2, k2, p2, k1, *k7, p2, k2, p2, k1* to last 17 sts, k7, p2, k2, p2, k4.

Row 14: P4, 2/2/2 LC, p7, *p1, 2/2/2 LC, p7* to last 11 sts, p1, 2/2/2 LC, p4.

Row 15: K4, p2, k2, p2, k1, *K7, p2, k2, p2, k1* to last 17 sts, k7, p2, k2, p2, k4.

Row 16: P3, k2tog, yo, k1, p2, k1, yo, ssk, p6, *k2tog, yo, k1, p2, k1, yo, ssk, p6* to last 11 sts, k2tog, yo, k1, p2, k1, yo, ssk, p3.

Row 17: K3, p3, k2, p3, *k6, p3, k2, p3* to last 17 sts, k6, p3, k2, p3, k3.

Row 18: P2, k2tog, yo, k2, p2, k2, yo, ssk, p4, k2tog, *yo, k2, p2, k2, yo, ssk, p4, k2tog* to last 10 sts, yo, k2, p2, k2, yo, ssk, p2.

Row 19: K2, p4, k2, p3, *p1, k4, p4, k2, p3* to last 17 sts, p1, k4, p4, k2, p4, k2.

Row 20: P1, k2tog, yo, k3, p2, k3, yo, ssk, p2, k2tog, yo, *k3, p2, k3, yo, ssk, p2, k2tog, yo* to last 11 sts, k3, p2, k3, yo, ssk, p1.

Row 21: K1, p5, k2, p3, *p2, k2, p5, k2, p3* to last 17 sts, p2, k2, p5, k2, p5, k1.

Row 22: P1, k3, k2tog, yo, p2, yo, ssk, k3, p2, k2, *k1, k2tog, yo, p2, yo, ssk, k3, p2, k2* to last 11 sts, k1, k2tog, yo, p2, yo, ssk, k3, p1.

Row 23: K1, p4, k4, p2, *p2, k2, p4, k4, p2* to last 17 sts, p2, k2, p4, k4, p4, k1.

Row 24: P1, k2, k2tog, yo, p4, yo, ssk, k2, p2, k2, *k2tog, yo, p4, yo, ssk, k2, p2, k2* to last 11 sts, k2tog, yo, p4, yo, ssk, k2, p1.

Row 25: K1, p3, k6, p1, *p2, k2, p3, k6, p1* to last 17 sts, p2, k2, p3, k6, p3, k1.

Row 26: P1, k1, k2tog, yo, p6, yo, ssk, k1, p2, k1, k2tog, *yo, p6, yo, ssk, k1, p2, k1, k2tog* to last 10 sts, yo, p6, yo, ssk, k1, p1.

Row 27 (WS): K1, p2, k8, *p2, k2, p2, k8* to last 17 sts, p2, k2, p2, k8, p2, k1.

Row 28 (RS): P1, k2, p8, 2/2/2 LC, *p8, 2/2/2 LC* to last 11 sts, p8, k2, p1.

Rep rows 1–28 for patt.

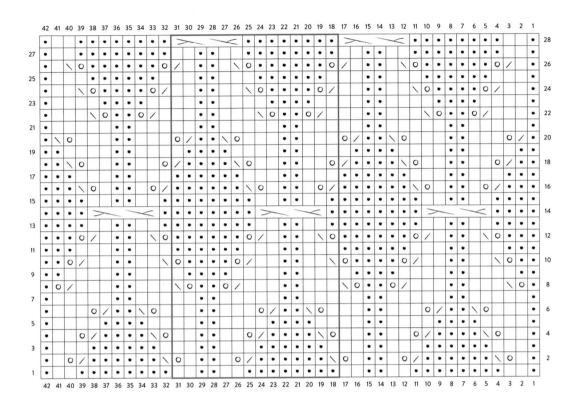

☐		RS: knit WS: purl
•		RS: purl WS: knit
O		yo
\		ssk
/		k2tog
☐		pattern repeat, repeat 7 times
⟩⟨		2/2/2 LC

FLORENTINA

Florentina is perfect for chilly spring days and summer nights.
It is a girly cardigan with a cable-knit look, but in reality, it is
an easy project for every knitter.

SIZES

0–3 mos (3–6 mos, 6–12 mos, 12–18 mos, 2 yr) (4 yr, 6 yr, 8 yr, 10 yr)
Recommended ease: 2″ / 5 cm of positive ease at chest

FINISHED MEASUREMENTS

Chest Circumference: 16 (18, 20, 22, 24) (26, 28, 30, 32)″ / 38 (43, 48, 53, 58) (63, 68, 73, 78) cm
Yoke Depth (front): 3.5 (4, 4.5, 5, 5) (5.5, 6, 6.5, 7)″ / 9 (10, 11, 13, 13) (14, 15, 16, 18) cm
Body Length to Underarm (front): 4 (4.5, 5, 5.5, 6) (7.5, 9, 10, 11)″ / 10 (11, 13, 14, 15) (19, 23, 25, 28) cm
Upper Arm Circumference: 6.5 (7, 8, 8.25, 9) (9.75, 10.5, 11, 11.25)″ / 16 (17, 20, 21, 23) (25, 26, 27, 28) cm
Sleeve Length to Underarm: 5.75 (6, 7, 8, 8.5) (10, 11.5, 13, 14)″ / 14 (15, 18, 20, 21) (25, 29, 33, 35) cm

MATERIALS

Yarn:
Pink version shown in size 4 yr on Ilana (height 38″ / 97 cm)
2 (2, 2, 2, 3) (3, 4, 4, 4) skeins of Tosh DK by Madeleinetosh (100% superwash merino wool, 225 yds / 205 m – 100 g), colourway Pink Mist Smoke Tree

Grey version shown in size 6 yr on Anja (height 47″ / 120 cm)
2 (2, 2, 2, 2) (3, 3, 4, 4) skeins of Merino DK by La Bien Aimée (100% merino, 252 yds / 230 m – 100 g), colourway Smoke

Or 238 (274, 346, 403, 452) (564, 672, 783, 879) yds / 218 (251, 317, 369, 414) (516, 615, 716, 804) m of DK-weight yarn

Needles: US 5 / 3.75 mm 16″ / 40 cm circular needles, 24″ / 60 cm and a set of DPNs. US 6 / 4 mm 16″ / 40 cm circular needles, 24″ / 60 cm and a set of DPNs

Notions: Stitch markers, stitch holders or waste yarn, tapestry needle, 5 (5, 6, 6, 7) (7, 7, 7, 8) small buttons

GAUGE

22 sts x 30 rows to 4″ / 10 cm on US 6 / 4 mm needles in St St, after blocking

NOTES

Sleeve instructions are written for DPNs. However, an alternate method of working small circumferences, such as Magic-Loop Method or short circular needles, can be used. As the yoke decreases, change to shorter circular needles when necessary.

The chart is read from bottom to top and from right to left on RS rows and from left to right on WS rows.

INSTRUCTIONS

The cardigan is worked from the bottom up with a circular yoke and a broken garter ridge pattern in the front and yoke. The sleeves are worked separately in the round to the base of the yoke, then joined. A section of short rows is worked at the back of the neck for a more comfortable fit.

SLEEVES

Using US 5 / 3.75 mm set of DPNs, CO 30 (30, 34, 34, 36) (38, 38, 40, 40) sts using the Long-Tail CO Method, or your preferred method. Join in the rnd making sure sts are not twisted. PM for BOR.

Rnd 1: *K1, p1* to end.
Work in 1 x 1 rib as est until work measures 1″ / 2.5 cm from CO edge.

Change to US 6 / 4 mm DPNs or preferred needles for small circumference knitting.
K 7 (5, 5, 5, 5) (3, 5, 7, 7) rnds.

SLEEVE INCREASES
Inc Rnd: K1, m1l, k to 1 st bef BOR m, m1r, k1. (2 sts inc'd)
Rep inc rnd every 10th (8th, 8th, 8th, 7th) (8th, 7th, 8th, 8th) rnd 2 (3, 4, 5, 6) (7, 9, 9, 10) more times. [36 (38, 44, 46, 50) (54, 58, 60, 62) sts]

Work in St St in the rnd until sleeve measures 5.75 (6, 7, 8, 8.5) (10, 11.5, 13, 14)" / 14 (15, 18, 20, 21) (25, 29, 33, 35) cm from CO edge, or desired length to underarm.

Next Rnd: K, ending 2 (2, 3, 3, 3) (3, 4, 4, 4) sts bef BOR m. Pl next 3 (3, 5, 5, 5) (5, 7, 7, 7) sts on waste yarn or st holder for underarm, RM when come to it. [33 (35, 39, 41, 45) (49, 51, 53, 55) sts]
Set aside first sleeve, pl rem 33 (35, 39, 41, 45) (49, 51, 53, 55) sts on waste yarn or spare needle.
Work second sleeve as first.

BODY

BOTTOM HEM
Using US 5 / 3.75 mm 24" / 60 cm circular needles, CO 83 (93, 105, 115, 127) (137, 149, 159, 171) sts using the Long-Tail CO Method, or your preferred method. You will continue to work flat.

Row 1: *K1, p1*to last st, k1.
Row 2: P1, *k1, p1*to end.
Rep rows 1 and 2 until work measures 1" / 2.5 cm from CO edge, ending on a row 2 and inc 1 st at centre of last row, using an m1l. [84 (94, 106, 116, 128) (138, 150, 160, 172) sts]

Change to US 6 / 4 mm 24" / 60 cm circular needles and work as foll:
Row 1 (RS): *P3, k2* 2 (2, 2, 3, 3) (3, 3, 3, 3) times, p3, PM, k to last 13 (13, 13, 18, 18) (18, 18, 18, 18) sts, PM, *p3, k2* 2 (2, 2, 3, 3) (3, 3, 3, 3) times, p3.
Row 2 (WS): *K3, p2* 2 (2, 2, 3, 3) (3, 3, 3, 3) times, k3, SM, p to last m, SM,*k3, p2* 2 (2, 2, 3, 3) (3, 3, 3, 3) times, k3.
Row 3: As row 1, slipping the m's.
Row 4: K13 (13, 13, 18, 18) (18, 18, 18, 18), SM, p to last m, SM, k to end.
Slipping the m's, rep rows 1–4 for Broken Garter Ridge Patt until work measures approx. 4 (4.5, 5, 5.5, 6) (7.5, 9, 10, 11)" / 10 (11.5, 12.75, 14, 15.25) (19, 23, 25.5, 28) cm from front CO edge or desired length to underarm ending with a row 4 of patt. RS is facing for next row.

JOIN FOR YOKE
Next Row: Work in Broken Garter Ridge Patt as est over first 13 (13, 13, 18, 18) (18, 18, 18, 18) sts, SM, k6 (8, 10, 8, 11) (13, 15, 18, 21) sts, pl next 3 (3, 5, 5, 5) (5, 7, 7, 7) sts on

waste yarn or st holder for right underarm. Transfer sts from one sleeve on to LHN of body, and k33 (35, 39, 41, 45) (49, 51, 53, 55) sts for right sleeve. K across next 40 (46, 50, 54, 60) (66, 70, 74, 80) back sts, pl next 3 (3, 5, 5, 5) (5, 7, 7, 7) sts onto waste yarn or st holder for left underarm. Transfer sts from rem sleeve on to LHN of body, and k33 (35, 39, 41, 45) (49, 51, 53, 55) sts for left sleeve. K to m, SM, work in Broken Garter Ridge Patt as est over last 13 (13, 13, 18, 18) (18, 18, 18, 18) sts. [144 (158, 174, 188, 208) (226, 238, 252, 268) sts in total: 19 (21, 23, 26, 29) (31, 33, 36, 39) sts for each front, 33 (35, 39, 41, 45) (49, 51, 53, 55) sts for each sleeve and 40 (46, 50, 54, 60,) (66, 70, 74, 80) sts for back.]

Working the Broken Garter Ridge Patt as est over the first and last 13 (13, 13, 18, 18) (18, 18, 18, 18) sts, work 1 row. You will have ended on row 2 of patt. RS is facing for next row.

Size 0–3 mos only
Adjustment Row (Dec) (RS): Work in patt as est over first 13 sts, SM, *k2tog* 3 times, *k1, k2tog* to 4 sts bef next m, *k2tog* twice, SM, work in patt as est to end. (103 sts)

Sizes 3–6 mos, 6–12 mos, 12–18 mos, 4 yr, 6 yr and 10 yr only
Adjustment Row (Dec) (RS): Work in patt as est to m, SM, k– (6, 3, 7, –) (3, 2, –, 5), *k2tog, k– (1, 1, 1, –) (1, 2, –, 2), k2tog, k– (1, 2, 2, –) (2, 2, –, 3)* to – (6, 5, 5, –) (5, 0, –, 2) sts bef next m, *k2tog* – (0, 1, 0, –) (1, 0, –, 0) time, k– (6, 3, 5, –) (3, 0, –, 2), SM, work in patt as est to end. [– (118, 133, 148, –) (173, 188, –, 218) sts]

Size 2 yr only
Adjustment Row (Dec) (RS): Work in patt as est to m, SM, k2tog, *k2tog, k1, k2tog, k2* to 2 sts bef next m, k2tog, SM, work in patt to end. (158 sts)

Size 8 yr only
Adjustment Row (Dec) (RS): Work in patt as est to m, k2tog, k2, *k2tog, k2, k2tog, k3* to 5 sts bef next m, k2tog, k1, k2tog, SM, work in patt as est to end. (203 sts)

All sizes resume
Work 1 (1, 1, 5, 5) (5, 5, 9, 9) row(s) in patt as est over the first and last 13 (13, 13, 18, 18) (18, 18, 18, 18) sts. You will have ended on a Row 4 of patt. RS is facing for next row.

peekaboo!

Beg to work Yoke as foll:

Row 1 (RS): *P3, k2* to last 3 sts, removing m's when come to them, and working the rem DSs as one (like a k2tog or a p2tog), p3.

Row 2 (WS): *K3, p2* to last 3 sts, k3.

Row 3: As row 1.

Row 4: K.

Rep rows 1–4 for Broken Garter Ridge Patt 0 (0, 1, 0, 0) (1, 2, 2, 3) more time(s).

Reading RS rows from right to left and WS rows from left to right, beg working from Chart as folls: Work row 9 (5, 5, 1, 1) (1, 1, 1, 1) of chart, working 5-st rep 20 (23, 26, 29, 31) (34, 37, 40, 43) times to last 3 sts, work last 3 sts as indicated on chart.

Next Row: Work first 3 sts as indicated on row 10 (6, 6, 2, 2) (2, 2, 2, 2) of chart, work 5-st rep 20 (23, 26, 29, 31) (34, 37, 40, 43) times to end of row.

Cont as est until the 23rd row of chart has been completed. [61 (70, 79, 88, 94) (103, 112, 121, 130) sts]

WORK BACK NECK SHAPING

Short Row 1 (WS): K48 (55, 61, 68, 73) (81, 88, 96, 105) sts, turn.

Short Row 2 (RS): MDS, bring yarn to back if knitting next st or bring yarn to front if purling next st, work in patt as est over next 37 (39, 42, 47, 51) (58, 63, 70, 79) sts, turn.

Short Row 3 (WS): MDS, bring yarn to back if knitting next st or bring yarn to front if purling next st, work in patt as est to 4 (4, 4, 4) (5, 5, 6, 6) sts bef the DS, turn.

Short Row 4 (RS): MDS, bring yarn to back if knitting next st or bring yarn to front if purling next st, work in patt as est to 4 (4, 4, 4) (5, 5, 6, 6) sts bef the DS, turn.

Next Row (WS): MDS, k to end of row, working the DSs as one (like a k2tog or a p2tog). [61 (70, 79, 79, 88) (94, 103, 112, 130) sts]

Adjustment Row (Dec) (RS): Work the rem DSs as one (like a k2tog or a p2tog), and at same time, k5 (7, 8, 4, 7) (10, 4, 9, 6), *k2tog, k6 (4, 3, 4, 4) (3, 4, 3, 3)* to last 0 (3, 6, 0, 3) (8, 0, 7, 4) sts, k to end. [54 (60, 66, 74, 80) (86, 94, 100, 106) sts]

NECKBAND

Using US 5 / 3.75 mm 24" / 60 cm circular needles, work as foll:

Row 1: *K1, p1* to end.

Cont in est 1 x 1 rib for 5 more rows.

BO evenly in 1 x 1 rib.

BUTTON BANDS

LEFT FRONT BUTTON BAND

With RS facing and using US 5 / 3.75 mm 24" / 60 cm circular needles, pick up and k46 (54, 56, 66, 66) (78, 90, 102, 104) sts (approx. 3 sts for every 4 rows) evenly down left front edge.

Row 1: *K1, p1* to end.

Cont in est 1 x 1 rib for 4 more rows.

BO evenly in 1 x 1 rib.

RIGHT FRONT BUTTONHOLE BAND

With RS facing and using US 5 / 3.75 mm 24" / 60 cm circular needles, pick up and k sts as bef, evenly up right front edge. [46 (54, 56, 66, 66) (78, 90, 102, 104) sts]

Row 1: *K1, p1* to end.

Rep row 1 once more.

Next Row (make buttonholes): K1, p1, *k2tog, yo, (k1, p1) 4 (5, 4, 5, 4) (5, 6, 7, 6) times*, rep from *–* 3 (3, 4, 4, 5) (5, 5, 5, 6) more times, k2tog, yo, k1, p1.

Rep row 1, 2 more times.

BO evenly in 1 x 1 rib.

FINISHING

Use 3-Needle Bind-Off or Grafting to join underarm sts. Weave in ends, closing any gaps that remain at the underarms. Sew buttons to correspond to buttonholes on left front button band. Block to measurements.

WRITTEN INSTRUCTIONS FOR CHART

*Sizes 12–18 mos, 2 yr, 4 yr, 6 yr, 8 yr and 10 yr
start here*
Row 1: *P3, k2* to last 3 sts, p3.
Row 2: K3, *p2, k3* to end.
Row 3: As row 1.
Row 4: K.

Sizes 3–6 mos and 6–12 mos start here
Row 5: As row 1.
Row 6: As row 2.
Row 7: As row 1.
Row 8: As row 4.

Size 0–3 mos starts here
Row 9: As row 1.
Row 10: As row 2.
Row 11: As row 1.
Row 12: As row 4.
Row 13: *P1, p2tog, k2* to last 3 sts, p2tog, p1.
Row 14: K2, *p2, k2* to end.
Row 15: *P2, k2* to last 2 sts, p2.
Row 16: K.
Row 17: As row 15.
Row 18: As row 14.
Row 19: As row 15.
Row 20: As row 16.
Row 21: *P2tog, k2* to last 2 sts, p2tog.
Row 22: K1, *p2, k1* to end.
Row 23: *P1, k2* to last st, p1.

YOKE CHART

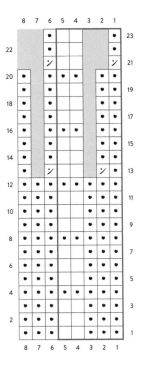

| | RS: knit
WS: purl |
| • | RS: purl
WS: knit |
⟋	p2tog
	pattern repeat
	no stitch

Note! Sizes 3–6 mos & 6–12 mos begin on row 5.
Size 0–3 mos begins on row 9. All other sizes begin
on row 1.

CIELO

This basic knit can be made with or without the crocheted
neckpiece, depending on your (or your child's) preference.
I chose to knit Cielo in a light blue colour that reminds me
of my childhood joys of waking up to a cloudless sky.

SIZES

0–3 mos (3–6 mos, 6–12 mos, 12–18 mos, 2 yr) (4 yr, 6 yr, 8 yr, 10 yr)
Recommended ease: 2" / 5 cm of positive ease
Shown in size 4 yr on Amanda (height 38" / 97 cm)

FINISHED MEASUREMENTS

Chest Circumference: 17 (19, 21, 23, 25) (27, 29, 31, 32)" / 43 (48, 53, 58, 63) (68, 73, 78, 80) cm
Yoke Depth (front): 3.75 (3.75, 4.5, 4.75, 4.75) (5.5, 6, 6.25, 7)" / 9 (10, 11, 12, 12) (14, 15, 16, 17) cm
Body Length to Underarm (front): 4 (4.5, 5, 5.5, 6) (7.5, 9, 10, 11)" / 10 (11, 13, 14, 15) (19, 23, 25, 28) cm
Upper Arm: 6.25 (6.5, 7, 7.5, 7.75) (8.5, 9.75, 10.25, 10.5)" / 16 (17 18, 19, 20) (22, 25, 26, 27) cm
Sleeve Length to Underarm: 5.75 (6, 7, 8, 8.5) (10, 11.5, 13, 14)" / 14 (15, 18, 20, 21) (25, 29, 33, 35) cm

MATERIALS

Yarn:
Sweater
2 (2, 2, 2, 2) (3, 3, 4, 4) skeins of Kid Classic by Rowan (70% lambswool, 22% kid mohair, 8% polyamide, 153 yds / 140 m – 50 g), colourway, Drought 876
Or 150 (150, 200, 250, 275) (350, 450, 525, 575) yds / 137 (137, 183, 229, 251) (320, 411, 480, 526) m of worsted-weight yarn

Collar (optional, version A and B)
1 skein of Spinni by Isager (100% wool, 330 yds / 301 m – 50 g), colourway 0

Needles: US 5 / 3.75 mm circular needles 16" / 40 cm (optional for sizes 4–10 yrs), 24" / 60 cm circular needles, and a set of DPNs. US 6 / 4 mm circular needles 16" / 40 cm (optional for sizes 4–10 yrs), 24" / 60 cm circular needles, and a set of DPNs. US 3 / 3 mm crochet hook for optional crochet collar

Notions: Stitch markers, stitch holders or waste yarn, tapestry needle, 1 small button for 5 smallest sizes for neckband

GAUGE

20 sts x 26 rnds to 4" / 10 cm on US 6 / 4 mm needles in St St, after blocking

NOTES

Neck and sleeve instructions are written for DPNs. However, an alternate method of working small circumferences, such as Magic-Loop Method or short circular needles, can be used. As the yoke increases, change to longer circular needles when necessary.

INSTRUCTIONS

The sweater is worked from the top down with a circular yoke. A section of short rows is worked at the bottom of the yoke for a better fit.

BODY

NECK EDGE
Using US 6 / 4 mm 16" / 40 cm circular needles, CO 60 (63, 66, 69, 72) (78, 81, 87, 90) sts using the Long-Tail CO Method, or your preferred method. Do not join in the rnd.

BEGIN BACK OPENING
Row 1: K.
Row 2: P.
Rep row 1 once more. Do not turn. Join in rnd. Pl BOR m (centre back neck).

BEGIN YOKE
Change to 24" / 60 cm circular needle when necessary.

Inc Rnd: K1, m1l, *k3, m1l* to last 2 sts, k2. [80 (84, 88, 92, 96) (104, 108, 116, 120) sts]
K 5 (5, 6, 6, 5) (6, 6, 7, 7) rnds
Inc Rnd: K2, m1l, *k4, m1l* to last 2 sts, k2. [100 (105, 110, 115, 120) (130, 135, 145, 150) sts]
K 5 (5, 6, 6, 5) (6, 6, 7, 7) rnds.
Inc Rnd: K3, m1l, *k5, m1l* to last 2 sts, k2. [120 (126, 132, 138, 144) (156, 162, 174, 180) sts]
K 5 (5, 6, 6, 5) (6, 6, 7, 7) rnds.
Inc Rnd: K4, m1l, *k6, m1l* to last 2 sts, k2. [140 (147, 154, 161, 168) (182, 189, 203, 210) sts]
K 4 (5, 6, 6, 5) (6, 6, 7, 7) rnds.

Size 0–3 mos only
Adjustment Rnd: K, dec 1 st across rnd. [139 sts]

Sizes 3–6 mos, 6–12 mos and 12–18 mos only
K – (0, 0, 2, –) (–, –, –, –) rnd(s).
Adjustment Rnd: K, inc – (2, 9, 16, –) (–, –, –, –) sts evenly spaced across rnd, using an m1l. [– (149, 163, 177, –) (–, –, –, –) sts]

Sizes 2 yr and 4 yr only
Inc Rnd: K5, m1l, *k7, m1l* to last 2 sts, k2. [– (–, –, –, 192) (208, –, –, –) sts]
K – (–, –, –, 5) (6, –, –, –) rnds.
Adjustment Rnd: K, dec – (–, –, –, 5) (3, –, –, –) sts evenly spaced across rnd. [– (–, –, –, 187) (205, –, –, –) sts]

Sizes 6 yr, 8 yr and 10 yr only
Inc Rnd: K5, m1l, *k7, m1l* to last 2 sts, k2. [– (–, –, –, –) (–, 216, 232, 240) sts]
K – (–, –, –, –) (–, 9, 7, 11) rnds.
Adjustment Rnd: K, inc – (–, –, –, –) (–, 11, 5, 6) sts evenly spaced across rnd, using an m1l. [– (–, –, –, –) (–, 227, 237, 246) sts]

All sizes resume
WORK BACK YOKE SHORT ROWS
Short Row 1 (RS): K35 (37, 41, 44, 47) (52, 57, 59, 62), turn.
Short Row 2 (WS): MDS, p to BOR, SM, p35 (37, 41, 44, 47) (52, 57, 59, 62), turn.
Short Row 3 (RS): MDS, SM, k to 5 (5, 5, 5, 6) (6, 7, 7, 8) sts bef the DS, turn.
Short Row 4 (WS): MDS, SM, p to 5 (5, 5, 5, 6) (6, 7, 7, 8) sts bef the DS, turn.
Short Row 5 (RS): MDS, k to 3 (3, 3, 3, 4) (4, 5, 5, 6) sts bef the DS, turn.
Short Row 6 (WS): MDS, p to 3 (3, 3, 3, 4) (4, 5, 5, 6) sts bef the DS, turn.
Rep short rows 5–6, 0 (0, 0, 0, 0) (0, 1, 1, 1) more time.

Next Rnd (RS): MDS, k back to BOR, SM, then k 1 rnd working the DSs as one (like a k2tog). [139 (149, 163, 177, 187) (205, 227, 237, 246) sts]

DIVIDE FOR BODY
Next Rnd: Leave BOR m in pl, k20 (22, 25, 27, 29) (32, 34, 36, 38), pl next 29 (30, 32, 34, 35) (39, 45, 46, 48) sts

for sleeve onto waste yarn or holder, using Backwards Loop Method, CO 2 (3, 3, 3, 4) (4, 4, 5, 5) sts for underarm, k41 (45, 49, 55, 59) (63, 69, 73, 74), pl next 29 (30, 32, 34, 35) (39, 45, 46, 48) sts for sleeve onto waste yarn or holder, using Backwards Loop Method, CO 2 (3, 3, 3, 4) (4, 4, 5, 5) sts for underarm, k to end. [85 (95, 105, 115, 125) (135, 145, 155, 160) sts]

Cont in St St in the rnd until body measures 3 (3.5, 4, 4.5, 5) (6.5, 8, 9, 10)" / 8 (9, 10, 11, 13) (16, 20, 23, 25) cm from underarm or 1" / 2.5 cm less than desired length to start of lower hem.

LOWER HEM
Change to US 5 / 3.75 mm circular needles and work as foll:
Rnd 1: *K1, p1* to end.
Rep rnd 1, 5 more times.
BO evenly in 1 x 1 rib.

SLEEVES

Pl 29 (30, 32, 34, 35) (39, 45, 46, 48) sts on waste yarn for sleeve onto US 6 / 4 mm set of DPNs or preferred style for working small circumferences, and beg at centre of underarm, pick up and k 1 (1, 1, 1, 2) (2, 2, 2, 2) st(s) along underarm CO sts, k29 (30, 32, 34, 35) (39, 45, 46, 48) sts from sleeve, and then pick up and k 1 (2, 2, 2, 2) (2, 2, 3, 3) st(s) along underarm CO to centre. PM for BOR. [31 (33, 35, 37, 39) (43, 49, 51, 53) sts]

Sizes 0–3 mos, 3–6 mos, 6–12 mos, 12–18 mos, 2 yr, 6 yr and 8 yr only
Adjustment Rnd: K1, ssk, k to end. [30 (32, 34, 36, 38) (–, 48, 50, –) sts]

Sizes 4 yr, 6 yr, 8 yr and 10 yr only
K 14 rnds.
Dec Rnd: K1, ssk, k to 3 sts from end, k2tog, k1. (2 sts dec'd)
Rep dec rnd every 14th rnd – (–, –, –, –) (1, 2, 3, 3) more time(s). [– (–, –, –, –) (39, 42, 42, 45) sts]

All sizes resume
Cont in St St in the rnd until sleeve measures 4.75 (5, 6, 7, 7.5) (9, 10.5, 12, 13)" / 12 (13, 15, 18, 19) (23, 26, 30, 33) cm from CO edge, or 1" / 2.5 cm less than desired length to start of sleeve cuff.

Adjustment Rnd: K0 (1, 2, 0, 1) (0, 0, 0, 0), *k1, k2tog* to last 0 (1, 2, 0, 1) (0, 0, 0, 0) sts, k to end. [20 (22, 24, 24, 26) (26, 28, 28, 30) sts]

SLEEVE CUFF

Change to US 5 / 3.75 mm set of DPNs and work as foll:
Rnd 1: *K1, p1* to end.
Rep rnd 1, 5 more times.
BO evenly in 1 x 1 rib.
Work second sleeve as first.

OPTIONAL COLLARS

COLLAR A

Shown on pages 152–156
(Multiple of 6 sts)
With US 3 / 3 mm crochet hook and single strand of crochet yarn, ch a multiple of 6 sts until the chain fits evenly around neck edge, just below the rolled edge. For a size 2, 72 ch were used.

Row 1 (RS): Ch5, 1 sc in 8th ch from hook, (ch3, sl st in first ch of ch3), ch4, skip next 2 base ch, *1 sc in next base ch, (ch3, sl st in first ch of ch3), ch4, skip next 2 base ch*, rep *–* to last 4 base ch, 1 sc in next base ch, (ch3, sl st in first ch of ch3), ch2, skip next 2 base ch, 1 dc in last base ch, turn.
Row 2: Ch1, 1 sc in top of dc, *ch4, 1 sc in next ch4 sp, (ch3, sl st in first ch of ch3)*, rep *–* to last sp, ch4, 1 sc in 3rd ch of last ch5 turning ch, turn.
Row 3: Ch5, 1 sc in first ch4 sp, (ch3, sl st in first ch of ch3), *ch4, 1 sc in next ch4 sp, (ch3, sl st in first ch of ch3)*, rep *–* to end, ch2, 1 dc in top of last sc, turn.
Row 4: Ch1, 1 sc in top of dc, *ch5, 1 sc in next ch4 sp, (ch3, sl st in first ch of ch3)*, rep *–* to last sp, ch5, 1 sc in 3rd ch of last ch5 turning ch, turn.
Row 5: Ch6, 1 sc in first ch5 sp, (ch3, sl st in first ch of ch3), *ch5, make Bobble in next ch5 sp as folls: [(yo, draw up a loop, yo, draw through 2 loops on hook) 5 times, yo, draw through all 6 loops on hook], ch5, 1 sc in next ch5 sp, (ch3, sl st in first ch of ch3)*, rep *–* to last ch5 space, ch5, make Bobble in last ch5 sp, ch6, 1 sc in top of last sc turn.
Row 6: Ch5, 1 sc in first ch6 sp, (ch3, sl st in first ch of ch3), *ch5, 1 sc in next ch5 sp, (ch3, sl st in first ch of ch3)*, rep *–* to last sp, ch5, 1 sc in 3rd ch of last ch6 turning ch.

Row 7: *Ch5, make Bobble in next ch5 sp, ch5, 1 sc in next ch5 sp, (ch3, sl st in first ch of ch3)*, rep *–* to last sp, ch5, make Bobble in last ch5 sp, ch 5, 1 sc in 3rd ch of ch5 turning ch, do not turn.
Cont to sl st evenly along side of collar, ending at neck edge. Fasten off.

COLLAR B

Shown on page 104
(Multiple of 3 sts)
With US 3 / 3 mm crochet hook and single strand of crochet yarn, ch a multiple of 3 sts until the chain fits evenly around neck edge, just below the rolled edge. Add 1 for base ch. For a 6–12 mos size, 85 ch were used (84 + 1).

Row 1 (RS): Ch5, work 1 sc in each st to end, turn.
Row 2: Ch3, 1 dc in first sc, *skip 2 sc, (1dc, ch2, 1dc) in next sc*, rep *-* to end, turn.
Row 3: Ch3, skip first ch2 sp, *(2dc, ch2, 2dc) in next ch2 sp*, rep *-* to last ch2 sp, (2dc, ch2, 2dc) in last ch2 sp, 1 dc in last dc, 1 dc in top of ch3 turning ch, turn.
Row 4: Ch3, 1 dc in next dc, *(2dc, ch2, 2dc) in next ch2 sp*, rep *-* to last ch2 sp, (2dc, ch2, 2dc) in last ch2 sp, 2 dc in top of ch3 turning ch, turn.
Row 5: Ch3, skip first dc, 1 dc in next dc, *(3dc, ch2, 3dc) in next ch2 sp*, rep *-* to last ch2 sp, (3dc, ch2, 3dc) in last ch2 sp, 2 dc in top of ch3 turning ch, turn.
Row 6: As row 5.
Row 7: (4dc, ch2, 4dc) in first ch2 sp, *(4dc, ch2, 4dc) in next ch2 sp*, rep *-* to last ch2 sp, (4dc, ch2, 4dc) in last ch2 sp, sl st in top of ch3 turning ch, do not turn. Cont to sl st evenly along side of collar, ending at neck edge. Fasten off.

BOTH COLLARS
Attaching Collar to Neck Edge
With RS of work facing, pl collar evenly under CO edge of neck, beg and ending at back opening. With US 5 / 3.75 mm 16" / 40 cm circular needles, pick up and k 1 row along the neck edge, while BO the row at same time as foll: Beg at the left back opening, pick up and k the first ch of the collar and the first st of the CO edge of the neck tog. *Pick up and k the next st ch of the collar (the ch that is at the base of the sc for Collar A or at the base of the [dc, ch1, dc] for Collar B) and the next st of the CO edge of the neck tog. Lift the 1st st over the 2nd st and off the RHN to BO. (Pick up and k the next st of the neck edge only, and BO) twice.* In a general way, ease the collar in place in this manner *-* until the collar ends at the right back opening. (ie. It may be that you need to pick up 1 or 3 sts along the neck edge rather than always picking up 2 sts in between in order to ease the collar in neatly.) Pick up and k 1 st in each of the last 2 sts through both the collar and neck while BO in same manner. Fasten off.

Note! To ease the collar in neatly, it may take more than 1 try. Be patient!

NECK EDGE
With US 5 / 3.75 mm 16" / 40 cm circular needles, RS of work facing, and beg at left back opening, pick up and k 1 st in each CO st evenly around neck edge. [60 (63, 66, 69, 72) (78, 81, 87, 90) sts]

Working back and forth on the circular needle, p 1 row.
Next Row: K2, yo, k2tog (for buttonhole), k to end.
Next Row: P.
BO evenly kwise.

FINISHING

If desired, with RS facing and crochet hook, sl st 1 row evenly around back opening. Fasten off. Weave in ends, closing any gaps that rem at the underarms. Sew button to correspond to buttonhole on neck band. Block to measurements.

ROBIN

Crochet is a popular craft in El Salvador, my home country,
as the weather is generally too hot for knitted clothes.
The neckpiece of this Robin cardigan is a relatively simple
project, but the result is equally charming without it.

SIZES

0–3 mos (3–6 mos, 6–12 mos, 12–18 mos, 2 yr) (4 yr, 6 yr, 8 yr, 10 yr)
Recommended ease: 2" / 5 cm of positive ease at chest
Shown in size 4 yr on Ilana (height 38" / 97 cm)

FINISHED MEASUREMENTS

Chest Circumference: 15.25 (17, 19.25, 21, 23.25) (25, 27.25, 29, 31.25)" / 38 (43, 48, 53, 58) (63, 68, 73, 78) cm
Yoke Depth (front): 3.5 (4, 4.5, 5, 5) (5.5, 6, 6.5, 7)" / 9 (10, 12, 13, 13) (14, 15, 17, 18) cm
Body Length to Underarm (at front): 3 (3.5, 4.25, 4.5, 5.5) (6, 6.5, 7, 7.5)" / 8 (9, 11, 11, 14) (15, 16, 18, 19) cm
Upper Arm Circumference: 6.5 (7, 8, 8.25, 9) (9.75, 10.5, 11, 11.25)" / 16 (17, 20, 21, 23) (25, 26, 27, 28) cm
Sleeve Length to Underarm: 5.75 (6, 7, 8, 8.5) (10, 11.5, 13, 14)" / 14 (15, 18, 20, 21) (25, 29, 33, 35) cm

MATERIALS

Yarn:

Yarn A: 2 (2, 2, 2, 3) (3, 4, 4, 5) skeins of Merino by Knitting for Olive (100% merino wool, 273 yds / 249 m – 50 g), colourway Rust
Or 340 (392, 495, 580, 667) (802, 926, 1069, 1187) yds / 311 (359, 453, 531, 610) (734, 847, 978, 1086) m of fingering-weight yarn

Yarn B: 2 (2, 2, 3, 3) (4, 4, 5, 5) skeins of Soft Silk Mohair by Knitting for Olive (70% mohair, 30% silk, 246 yds / 225 m – 25 g), colourway Rust
Or 340 (392, 495, 580, 667) (802, 926, 1069, 1187) yds / 311 (359, 453, 531, 610) (734, 847, 978, 1086) m of lace-weight yarn

Both yarns are held together throughout the pattern with the exception of the collar. Collar is worked with 1 strand of Yarn A, fingering-weight.

Needles: US 5 /3.75 mm 16" / 40 cm circular needles (optional), 24" / 60 cm and a set of DPNs. US 6 / 4 mm 16" / 40 cm circular needles (optional), 24" / 60 cm and a set of DPNs. US 3-D / 3.25 mm crochet hook for crocheted collar.

Notions: Stitch markers, stitch holders or waste yarn, tapestry needle, 5 (5, 6, 6, 7) (7, 7, 7, 7) small buttons.

GAUGE

22 sts x 30 rows to 4" / 10 cm on US 6 / 4 mm needles in St St, after blocking.

NOTES

Sleeve instructions are written for DPNs. However, an alternate method of working small circumferences, such as Magic-Loop Method or short circular needles, can be used for the larger sizes. As the yoke increases, change to longer circular needles when necessary.

INSTRUCTIONS

The cardigan is worked from the top down with a circular yoke. A small section of short rows is worked at the back of the neck and above the hem for a more comfortable fit. The collar is crocheted separately and attached to the neck by picking up 1 st from neck edge and 1 st from collar and knitting the 2 sts together while easing the collar along the neck edge as you work.

NECKBAND

With US 5 / 3.75 mm 24" / 60 cm circular needles and a strand of each yarn A and B held together, CO 55 (61, 67, 75, 79) (87, 91, 95, 101) sts using the Long-Tail CO Method, or your preferred method. You will continue to work flat.

K 1 row.
P 1 row.

Change to US 6 / 4 mm 24" / 60 cm circular needles and work as foll:

Sizes 0–3 mos, 3–6 mos, 6–12 mos, 12–18 mos, 2 yr, 4 yr and 8 yr only
Adjustment Row: K10 (9, 9, 5, 9) (3, –, 8, –), *m1l, k9 (7, 6, 5, 4) (6, –, 3, –)* to last 0 (3, 4, 0, 6) (0, –, 6, –) st(s), k0 (3, 4, 0, 6) (0, –, 6, –). [60 (68, 76, 89, 95) (101, –, 122, –) sts]

Sizes 6 yr and 10 yr only

Adjustment Row: K– (–, –, –, –) (–, 7, –, 2), *m1l, k3, m1l, k4* to last – (–, –, –, –) (–, 7, –, 1) st(s), m1l, k– (–, –, –, –) (–, 7, –, 1). [– (–, –, –, –) (–, 114, –, 130) sts]

All sizes resume

WORK BACK NECK SHAPING

Short Row 1 (WS): P48 (54, 58, 66, 73) (80, 87, 97, 105), turn.

Short Row 2 (RS): MDS, k35 (39, 39, 42, 50) (58, 59, 71, 79), turn.

Short Row 3 (WS): MDS, p to 4 (4, 4, 4, 4) (5, 5, 5, 6) sts bef the DS, turn.

Short Row 4 (RS): MDS, k to 4 (4, 4, 4, 4) (5, 5, 5, 6) sts bef the DS, turn.

Rep short rows 3 and 4, 1 (1, 1, 1, 2) (2, 2, 3, 3) more time(s).

Next Row (WS): MDS, p to end of row, working the DSs as one (like a p2tog). [60 (68, 76, 89, 95) (101, 114, 122, 130) sts]

Sizes 0–3 mos, 3–6 mos and 6–12 mos only

Inc Row: K2, *m1l, k2* to end, and at same time, work the rem DSs as one (like a k2tog). [89 (101, 113, –, –) (–, –, –, –) sts]

Next Row: P.

Work 6 (6, 8, –, –) (–, –, –, –) rows in St St.

Inc Row: K2, *m1l, k3* to end. [118 (134, 150, –, –) (–, –, –, –) sts]

Next Row: P.

Work 6 (6, 8, –, –) (–, –, –, –) rows in St St.

Inc Row: K3, *m1l, k4* to last 3 sts, m1l, k3. [147 (167, 187, –, –) (–, –, –, –) sts]

Next Row: P.

Work 4 (8, 8, –, –) (–, –, –, –) rows in St St.

Sizes 12–18 mos, 2 yr and 4 yr only

Inc Row: K2, *m1l, k3* to end, and at same time, work the rem DSs as one (like a k2tog). [– (–, –, 118, 126) (134, –, –, –) sts]

Next Row: P.

Work – (–, –, 6, 6) (8, –, –, –) rows in St St.

Inc Row: K3, *m1l, k4* to last 3 sts, m1l, k3. [– (–, –, 147, 157) (167, –, –, –) sts]

Next Row: P.

Work – (–, –, 6, 6) (8, –, –, –) rows in St St.

Inc Row: K3, *m1l, k5* to last 4 sts, m1l, k4. [– (–, –, 176,

188) (200, –, –, –) sts]

Next Row: P.

Work – (–, –, 6, 6) (8, –, –, –) rows in St St.

Inc Row: K4, *m1l, k6* to last 4 sts, m1l, k4. [– (–, –, 205, 219) (233, –, –, –) sts]

Next Row: P.

Work – (–, –, 8, 8) (6, –, –, –) rows in St St.

Sizes 6 yr, 8 yr and 10 yr only

Inc Row: K3, *m1l, k4* to last 3 sts, m1l, k3, and at same time, work the rem DSs as one (like a k2tog). [– (–, –, –, –) (–, 142, 152, 162) sts]

Next Row: P.

Work – (–, –, –, –) (–, 6, 6, 8) rows in St St.

Inc Row: K3, *m1l, k5* to last 4 sts, m1l, k4. [– (–, –, –, –) (–, 170, 182, 194) sts]

Next Row: P.

Work – (–, –, –, –) (–, 6, 6, 8) rows in St St.

Inc Row: K4, *m1l, k6* to last 4 sts, m1l, k4. [– (–, –, –, –) (–, 198, 212, 226) sts]

Next Row: P.

Work – (–, –, –, –) (–, 6, 6, 8) rows in St St.

Inc Row: K4, *m1l, k7* to last 5 sts, m1l, k5. [– (–, –, –, –) (–, 226, 242, 258) sts]

Next Row: P.

Work – (–, –, –, –) (–, 6, 6, 8) rows in St St.

Inc Row: K5, *m1l, k8* to last 5 sts, m1l, k5. [– (–, –, –, –) (–, 254, 272, 290) sts]

Next Row: P.

Work – (–, –, –, –) (–, 8, 10, 6) rows in St St.

All sizes resume

Adjustment Row: K, dec 3 (9, 9, 13, 11) (7, 12, 16, 18) sts evenly spaced around. [144 (158, 178, 192, 208) (226, 242, 256, 272) sts]

P 1 row.

DIVIDE FOR BODY

Next Row (RS): K19 (22, 24, 27, 29) (32, 34, 37, 40), pl next 33 (35, 40, 42, 45) (49, 52, 54, 56) sts from left sleeve on waste yarn, using Backwards Loop Method, CO 3 (3, 4, 4, 5) (5, 6, 6, 6) sts for left underarm, k across next 40 (44, 50, 54, 60) (64, 70, 74, 80) sts for back, pl next 33 (35, 40, 42, 45) (49, 52, 54, 56) sts from right sleeve on waste yarn, using Backwards Loop Method, CO 3 (3, 4, 4, 5) (5, 6, 6, 6) sts for right underarm, k to end. [84 (94, 106, 116, 128) (138, 150, 160, 172) sts]

Next Row: P21 (23, 26, 29, 32) (34, 37, 40, 43), PM for side, p42 (48, 54, 58, 64) (70, 76, 80, 86), PM for side, p to end.

Work in St St until body measures approx. 2.25 (2.75, 3.5, 3.75, 4.75) (5.25, 5.5, 6, 6.5)" / 6 (7, 9, 9, 12) (13, 14, 15, 16) cm from underarm or 0.75 (0.75, 0.75, 0.75, 0.75) (0.75, 1, 1, 1)" / 2 (2, 2, 2, 2) (2, 3, 3, 3) cm less than desired length to start of lower hem, ending with a WS row.

WORK LOWER BACK SHAPING

Short Row 1 (RS): K to first m, SM, k to next m, SM, k3 (3, 3, 3, 3) (5, 5, 5, 6), turn.
Short Row 2 (WS): MDS, p to first m, SM, p to next m, SM, p3 (3, 3, 3, 3) (5, 5, 5, 6), turn.
Short Row 3 (RS): MDS, SM, k to 4 (4, 4, 4, 4) (7, 7, 7, 8) sts bef the DS, turn.
Short Row 4 (WS): MDS, p to 4 (4, 4, 4, 4) (7, 7, 7, 8) sts bef the DS, turn.
Rep short rows 3 and 4, 0 (0, 0, 0, 1) (1, 1, 2, 2) more time(s).

Next Row (RS): MDS, k to end, working the DSs as one (like a k2tog). [84 (94, 106, 116, 128) (138, 150, 160, 172) sts]
Next Row (WS): K, inc 1 st at centre back using an m1l, and at same time, work the rem DSs as one (like a k2tog). [85 (95, 107, 117, 129) (139, 151, 161, 173) sts]

LOWER HEM

With US 5 / 3.75 mm 24" / 60 cm circular needles and work as foll:
Row 1: *K1, p1* to last st, k1.
Row 2: P1, *k1, p1* to end.
Rep rows 1–2, 2 (2, 2, 2, 2) (2, 3, 3, 3) more times.
BO evenly in rib patt.

SLEEVES

Pl 33 (35, 40, 42, 45) (49, 52, 54, 56) sts on waste yarn for right sleeve onto US 6 / 4 mm set of DPNs or preferred style for working small circumferences, and beg at centre of underarm, pick up and k 1 (1, 2, 2, 2) (2, 3, 3, 3) st(s) along underarm CO sts, k34 (34, 38, 42, 46) (50, 54, 54, 58) sts from sleeve, and then pick up and k 2 (2, 2, 2, 3) (3, 3, 3, 3) sts along underarm CO to centre. PM for BOR. [36 (38, 44, 46, 50) (54, 58, 60, 62) sts]

Work 7 (5, 4, 8, 7) (9, 6, 9, 9) rnds in St St.

Dec Rnd: K1, ssk, k to last 3 sts, k2tog, k1. (2 sts dec'd)
Rep dec rnd every 10th (8th, 8th, 8th, 8th) (8th, 8th, 8th, 8th) rnd 2 (3, 4, 3, 2) (4, 3, 7, 8) more times, then every 0 (0, 0, 6th, 6th) (6th, 6th, 6th, 6th) rnd 0 (0, 0, 2, 4) (3, 6, 2, 2) more time(s). [30 (30, 34, 34, 36) (38, 38, 40, 40) sts]

If necessary, work even in St St in the rnd until sleeve measures 5 (5.25, 6.25, 7.25, 7.75) (9.25, 10.5, 12, 13)" / 13 (13, 16, 18, 19) (23, 26, 30, 33) cm or 0.75 (0.75, 0.75, 0.75, 0.75) (0.75, 1, 1, 1)" / 2 (2, 2, 2, 2) (2, 3, 3, 3) cm less than desired length to start of sleeve cuff.

Next Rnd: P.

SLEEVE CUFF

With US 5 / 3.75 mm set of DPNs, work as foll:
Rnd 1: *K1, p1* to end.
Cont in est 1 x 1 rib for 5 (5, 5, 5, 5) (5, 7, 7, 7) more rnds.
BO evenly in 1 x 1 rib patt.

Work second sleeve as first.

BUTTON BANDS

LEFT FRONT BUTTON BAND

With RS facing and using US 5 / 3.75 mm 24" / 60 cm circular needles, pick up and k 38 (46, 48, 54, 62) (66, 70, 76, 82) sts evenly down left front edge (approx. 3 sts for every 4 rows).

Row 1 (WS): K.
Rep row 1, 2 more times.
BO evenly kwise.

RIGHT FRONT BUTTONHOLE BAND

With RS facing and using US 5 / 3.75 mm 24" / 60 cm circular needles, pick up and k sts as bef, evenly up right front edge. [38 (46, 48, 54, 62) (66, 70, 76, 82) sts]

Row 1 (WS): K.
Next Row (make buttonholes): K5 (5, 3, 4, 3) (7, 5, 5, 5), *k2tog, yo, k5 (7, 6, 7, 7) (7, 8, 9, 10)*, rep *–* 3 (3, 4, 4, 5) (5, 5, 5, 5) more times, k2tog, yo, k3.
Next Row: As row 1.
BO evenly kwise.

CROCHET COLLAR

(Multiple of 3 sts)
With US 3-D / 3.25 mm crochet hook and 1 strand of Yarn A, ch a multiple of 3 sts until chain fits evenly along neck edge, beg 1 or 2 sts in from the inside edge of the front bands. Add 1 st for base ch. For a size 4 yr, we used 103 ch (102 + 1).

Row 1 (RS): Ch1, work 1 sc in each st to end, turn.
Row 2: Ch3, 1 dc in first sc, *skip 2 sc, (1dc, ch2, 1dc) in next sc*, rep *–* to end, turn.
Row 3: Ch3, (1dc, ch2, 2dc) in first ch2 sp, *(2dc, ch2, 2dc) in next ch2 sp*, rep *–* to end, turn.
Row 4: As row 3.
Row 5: Skip first dc, sl st in top of next dc, ch3, (1dc, ch2, 2dc) in first ch2 sp, *(2dc, ch2, 2dc) in next ch2 sp*, rep *–* to end, turn.
Row 6: Skip first dc, sl st in top of next dc, ch3, (2dc, ch2, 3dc) in first ch2 sp, *(3dc, ch2, 3dc) in next ch2 sp*, rep *–* to end, turn.
Row 7: Skip first dc, sl st in top of each of next 2dc, ch3, (2dc, ch2, 3dc) in first ch2 sp, *(3dc, ch2, 3dc) in next ch2 sp*, rep *–* to end, turn.
Row 8: As row 7.
Row 9: Skip first dc, sl st in top of each of next 2dc, ch3, (2dc, ch1, 3dc) in first ch2 sp, *(3dc, ch1, 3dc) in next ch2 sp*, rep *–* to end. Break yarn and fasten off.

ATTACHING COLLAR TO CARDIGAN
With RS of collar and cardigan facing, pl neck edge of collar evenly along neck edge of cardigan, aligning edges of collar 1 or 2 sts in from the inside edge of the front button bands. Pin gently into position if desired. Using US 5 / 3.75 mm 24" / 60 cm circular needles and a strand of each yarn A and B held together, pick up and k 4 sts evenly across top of buttonhole band, pick up first st from the collar and parallel st from neckband of cardigan and k them tog (5 sts on RHN). Cont in this manner picking up 1 st in each st of neck edge along the cardigan and at same time, easing the collar in pl (skipping every few sts of collar as needed) until all sts of cardigan neckband have been picked up and crochet collar fits neatly along the neck edge, At inside edge of left button band, pick up and k 4 sts across top of button band. You should have approx. 63 (69, 75, 83, 87) (95, 99, 103, 109) sts. However, the exact number of sts

you end up with does not matter as long as the collar fits neatly along the neckband.

Next Row (WS): K.
BO evenly kwise.

FINISHING

Weave in ends, closing any gaps that remain at the underarms. Sew buttons to correspond to buttonholes on left front button band. Block to measurements.

KIELO

The droplets running down the socks are like lilies of the valley: little bells spreading their sweet scent. Lily of the valley — or 'kielo' — is the national flower of Finland, the home of my publisher. For these socks, I also used Finnish yarn.

SIZES

6–9 mos (12–18 mos, 2–4 yrs, 6 yr, 8–10 yrs)

FINISHED MEASUREMENTS

Foot Circumference: 5 (6, 7, 7, 8)″ / 13 (15, 18, 18, 20) cm
Leg Length: 6.5 (7.5, 8.5, 9.5, 10.5)″ / 17 (19, 22, 24, 27) cm
Foot Length: 4.75 (5.25, 5.75, 6.5, 7.5)″ / 12 (14, 15, 17, 19) cm

MATERIALS

Yarn: 2 skeins of Sock by Tukuwool (80% Finnish wool, 20% nylon, 175 yds / 160 m – 50 g), colourway Aava H31 Or 140 (190, 248, 279, 359) yds / 128 (174, 227, 255, 328) m of fingering-weight yarn

Needles: US 3 / 3.25 mm set of DPNs

Notions: Removable stitch markers, stitch holder or waste yarn, tapestry needle

GAUGE

24 sts x 36 rows to 4″ / 10 cm on US 3 / 3.25 mm needles in St St, after blocking

20 sts x 40 rows to 4″ / 10 cm on US 3 / 3.25 mm needles in Lace Stitch Patt, after blocking

STITCH PATTERNS

LACE STITCH PATTERN (MULTIPLE OF 5 STS)
Rnd 1: *K3, yo, ssk* to end.
Rnd 2: K.
Rnd 3: *K3, k2tog, yo* to end.
Rnd 4: K.
Rep rnds 1–4 for patt.

NOTES

Instructions are written for DPNs. However, an alternate method of working small circumferences, such as Magic-Loop Method, can be used. If using Magic-Loop Method, place a marker for each needle change when setting up gusset.

Foot length is adjustable.

INSTRUCTIONS

The socks are knit from the cuff down to the toe. The heel is shaped using the heel flap method and the toe is grafted together.

CUFF

Using US 3 / 3.25 mm set of DPNs, CO 24 (28, 32, 36, 40) sts using the Long-Tail CO Method, or your preferred method. Evenly disperse sts over 4 DPNs. Join in the rnd making sure sts are not twisted. Pl a removable m for BOR.

Rnd 1: *K2, p2* to end.
Cont in est 2 x 2 rib for 6 more rnds.

Sizes 6–9 mos, 12–18 mos, 2–4 yrs and 8–10 yrs only
Work 1 rnd in 2 x 2 rib as est and at same time, inc 1 (2, 3, –, 0) st(s) evenly spaced around, using an m1l. [25 (30, 35, –, 40) sts]

Size 6 yr only
Next Rnd: *K2, p2* to last 4 sts, k2, p2tog. [– (–, –, 35, –) sts]

LEG

Rep rnds 1–4 for Lace Stitch Patt (See Stitch Patt) until work from CO edge measures approx. 6.5 (7.5, 8.5, 9.5, 10.5)″ / 16 (19, 21, 24, 26) cm or desired length to start of heel flap, ending on a rnd 3 of lace patt.

HEEL FLAP

Next Row: K13 (13, 18, 18, 18), and turn work. Arrange the 13 (13, 18, 18, 18) sts just worked onto a single DPN. RM for BOR, and sl rem 12 (17, 17, 17, 22) sts onto a st holder or second DPN. You will now be working back and forth on just the heel sts.
Next Row (WS): Sl1 pwise wyif, p to end.
Row 1 (RS): *Sl1 pwise wyib, k1* to end.
Row 2 (WS): Sl1 pwise wyif, p to end.
Rep rows 1 and 2, 3 (3, 7, 7, 7) more times.

TURN HEEL

Working on the 13 (13, 18, 18, 18) heel flap sts, cont as foll:
Row 1 (RS): Sl 1 pwise wyib, k5 (5, 8, 8, 8), ssk, k1, turn.
Row 2 (WS): Sl 1 pwise wyif, p0 (0, 1, 1, 1), p2tog, p1, turn.
Row 3 (RS): Sl 1 pwise wyib, k to 1 st before the gap, ssk, k1, turn.
Row 4 (WS): Sl 1 pwise, wyif, p to 1 st before the gap, p2tog, p1, turn.
Rep rows 3 and 4 until all of the sts have been worked. You will have ended with a row 4. Turn. [7 (7, 10, 10, 10) sts]

SHAPE GUSSET

With RS facing, and using the DPN for the heel sts, pick up and k 5 (5, 9, 9, 9) sts into the slipped sts along the side of the heel flap (this is N1), pl sts from st holder back onto needle, and with a new DPN, k across the 12 (17, 17, 17, 22) instep sts (this is N2), with a new DPN, pick up and k 5 (5, 9, 9, 9) sts into the slipped sts along the second side of the heel flap, then with the same DPN, k3 (3, 5, 5, 5) from the heel (this is N3). Sts are dispersed over 3 DPNs and the centre of the heel is the BOR. [29 (34, 45, 45, 50) sts in total: 9 (9, 14, 14, 14) sts on N1, 12 (17, 17, 17, 22) sts on N2 and 8 (8, 14, 14, 14) sts on N3]

Dec Rnd: N1 – K to last 3 sts, k2tog, k1. N2 – Work rnd 1 of Lace Stitch Patt as est over 12 (17, 17, 17, 22) sts. N3 – K1, ssk, k to end. (2 sts dec'd)
Next Rnd: K.
Next Rnd: N1 – K to last 3 sts, k2tog, k1. N2 – Work rnd 3 of Lace Stitch Patt as est over 12 (17, 17, 17, 22) sts. N3 – K1, ssk, k to end. (2 sts dec'd)
Next Rnd: K.
Rep last 4 rnds 0 (0, 1, 1, 1) more time. [25 (30, 37, 37, 42) sts]
Rep first 2 rnds 0 (0, 1, 1, 1) more time. [25 (30, 35, 35, 40) sts]

Cont in patt as est, that is, work in Lace Stitch Patt on N2 and St St on N1 and N3 until work measures 3.5 (4, 4.25, 5, 6)" / 9 (10, 11, 13, 15) cm from back of heel or 1.25 (1.25, 1.5, 1.5, 1.5)" / 3 (3, 4, 4, 4) cm less than desired length when slightly stretched and ending with a rnd 1 or 3 of Lace Stitch Patt.

SHAPE TOE
Dec Rnd: N1 – K to last 3 sts, ssk, k1. N2 – K1, k2tog, k to last 3 sts, ssk, k1. N3 – K1, ssk, k to end. (4 sts dec'd)

Next Rnd: K.
Rep last 2 rnds 3 (4, 5, 5, 6) more times. [9 (10, 11, 11, 12) sts]

Sizes 6–9 mos, 2–4 yrs and 6 yr only
Next Rnd: K, dec 1 st in centre with k2tog, k to end. [8 (–, 10, 10, –) sts]

All sizes resume
Pl sts on N1 and N3 onto single DPN. There should now be an equal number of sts on each DPN.

FINISHING

Break yarn leaving a long tail and Graft 4 (5, 5, 5, 6) sts on each needle tog.

Work second sock as first.

Weave in ends and block to measurements.

It is not hard to guess where the name of this sweater comes from — my most prized childhood possession, a kaleidoscope. I wanted to turn all those reflective colours and shapes into a lovely pullover, making the everyday more exciting.

KALEIDOSCOPE

SIZES

0–3 mos (3–6 mos, 6–12 mos, 12–18 mos, 2 yr) (4 yr, 6 yr, 8 yr, 10 yr)
Recommended ease: 2" / 5 cm of positive ease at chest

FINISHED MEASUREMENTS

Chest Circumference: 17.25 (19, 21, 23, 25) (27, 29, 31, 33)" / 43 (48, 52, 57, 63) (68, 72, 77, 83) cm
Yoke Depth (front): 3.75 (4, 4.5, 5, 5) (5.5, 6, 6.5, 7)" / 9 (10, 11, 13, 13) (14, 15, 16, 18) cm
Body Length to Underarm (front): 4 (4.5, 5, 5.5, 6) (7, 8, 9, 10)" / 10 (11, 13, 14, 15) (18, 20, 23, 25) cm
Upper Arm Circumference: 6.25 (6.75, 7.5, 7.75, 8.25) (9, 10, 10.5, 10.75)" / 16 (17, 19, 19, 21) (23, 25, 26, 27) cm
Sleeve Length to Underarm: 5.75 (6.25, 7, 8.75, 8.75) (10.25, 11.5, 13, 14.25)" / 14 (16, 18, 22, 22) (26, 29, 33, 36) cm

MATERIALS

Yarn:
Pink version shown in size 4 yr on Amanda (height 38" / 97 cm)
Loch Lomond by BC Garn (100% GOTS certified organic wool, 170 yds / 155 m – 100 g)
1 (1, 1, 1, 2) (2, 2, 2, 3) skein(s) of Salmon 22 (A)
1 skein of each Copper 09 (B), Light Blue 10 (C), Beige 13 (D)

Blue version shown in size 6 yr on Anja (height 47" / 120 cm)
1 (1, 1, 1, 2) (2, 2, 2, 3) skein(s) of Denim Blue 16 (A)
1 skein of each Nougat 04 (B), Sand 19 (C), Beige 13 (D)

Or approx. the foll amounts of light worsted weight yarn:
100 (116, 141, 169, 189) (232, 308, 321, 367) yds / 90 (105, 128, 154, 172) (211, 281, 292, 335) m of A
13 (15, 16, 19, 21) (25, 29, 33, 38) yds / 12 (14, 15, 17, 19) (23, 26, 30, 34) m of B
7 (8, 9, 11, 12) (15, 17, 19, 22) yds / 6 (7, 9, 10, 11) (13, 15, 18, 20) m of C
11 (12, 19, 22, 24) (29, 34, 39, 44) yds / 10 (11, 17, 21, 22) (27, 31, 35, 41) of D

Needles: US 5 / 3.75 mm 16" / 40 cm circular needles (optional for sizes 2–10 yrs), 24" / 60 cm and a set of DPNs. US 6 / 4 mm 16" / 40 cm circular needles (optional for sizes 2–10 yrs), 24" / 60 cm and a set of DPNs

Notions: Stitch marker, waste yarn or stitch holders, tapestry needle, 1 button (four smallest sizes only)

GAUGE

21 sts x 30 rows to 4" / 10 cm on US 6 / 4 mm needles in St St, after blocking.

NOTES

Sleeve instructions are written for DPNs. However, an alternate method of working small circumferences, such as Magic-Loop Method or short circular needles, can be used. As the yoke decreases, change to shorter circular needles when necessary. Four smallest sizes have a button closure at back neck and will require a button.

The chart is read from bottom to top and from right to left when knitting in the rnd. When working stranded colourwork, keep floats in the back loose to maintain stretch. For floats longer than 5 sts, twist yarns together in the back.

INSTRUCTIONS

The pullover is worked from the bottom up with a circular yoke. The sleeves are knit separately in the round to the base of the yoke, then joined. A section of short rows is worked at the bottom of the back yoke for a more comfortable fit.

SLEEVES

Using US 5 / 3.75 mm set of DPNs and A, CO 28 (28, 32, 32, 34) (36, 36, 38, 38) sts using the Long-Tail CO Method, or your preferred method. Join in the rnd making sure sts are not twisted. PM for BOR.

Rnd 1: *K1, p1* to end.
Work in 1 x 1 rib as est until work measures 1" / 2.5 cm from CO edge, and inc 1 st at centre of last row. [29 (29, 33, 33, 35) (37, 37, 39, 39) sts]

Change to US 6 / 4 mm set of DPNs or preferred needles for small circumference knitting.
K 9 rnds.

SLEEVE INCREASES
Inc Rnd: K1, m1l, k to 1 st bef BOR m, m1r, k1. (2 sts inc'd)
Rep inc rnd every 10th (10th, 12th, 12th, 12th) (12th, 8th, 10th, 10th) rnd 1 (2, 2, 3, 3) (4, 7, 7, 8) more time(s). [33 (35, 39, 41, 43) (47, 53, 55, 57) sts]

Work in St St in the rnd until sleeve measures 5.75 (6.25, 7, 8.75, 8.75) (10.25, 11.5, 13, 14.25)" / 14 (16, 18, 22, 22) (26, 29, 33, 36) cm from CO edge, or desired length to underarm.

Next Rnd: K, ending 2 (2, 3, 3, 3) (3, 4, 4, 4) sts bef BOR m.

Pl next 3 (3, 5, 5, 5) (5, 7, 7, 7) sts on waste yarn or st holder for underarm, removing m when come to it.
Break yarn.
Set aside first sleeve, pl rem 30 (32, 34, 36, 38) (42, 46, 48, 50) sts on waste yarn or spare needle.
Work second sleeve as first.

BODY

Using US 5 / 3.75 mm 16" / 40 cm circular needles (or longer for sizes 2–10 yrs), and A, CO 90 (100, 110, 120, 132) (142, 152, 162, 174) sts using the Long-Tail CO Method, or your preferred method. Join in the rnd making sure sts are not twisted. PM for BOR.

Rnd 1: *K1, p1* to end.
Work in 1 x 1 rib as est until work measures 1" / 2.5 cm from CO edge.

Change to US 6 / 4 mm 16" / 40 cm circular needles (or longer for sizes 2–10 yrs).

Work in St St in the rnd until work measures 4 (4.5, 5, 5.5, 6) (7, 8, 9, 10)" / 10 (11.5, 12.75, 14, 15.25) (17.75, 20.25, 23, 25.5) cm from CO edge or desired length to underarm and ending 2 (2, 3, 3, 3) (3, 4, 4, 4) sts bef BOR m.

JOIN FOR YOKE
Next Rnd: K next 3 (3, 5, 5, 5) (5, 7, 7, 7) sts, then pl these sts on waste yarn for right underarm, removing BOR m. K across 42 (47, 50, 55, 61) (66, 69, 74, 80) sts of back, pl next 3 (3, 5, 5, 5) (5, 7, 7, 7) sts on waste yarn for underarm. Transfer sts from first sleeve on to LHN of body, and k30 (32, 34, 36, 38) (42, 46, 48, 50) sts for left sleeve, then k across front sts to end. Transfer sts from second sleeve on to LHN of body and k30 (32, 34, 36, 38) (42, 46, 48, 50) sts for right sleeve. PM for new BOR (right back shoulder). [144 (158, 168, 182, 198) (216, 230, 244, 260) sts]

K 1 rnd.

WORK BACK YOKE SHORT ROWS
Short Row 1 (RS): K57 (63, 67, 73, 80) (87, 92, 98, 105), turn.
Short Row 2 (WS): MDS, p to BOR m, SM, p15 (16, 17, 18, 19) (21, 23, 24, 25), turn.
Short Row 3 (RS): MDS, slipping BOR m, k to 2 (2, 3, 3, 3) (5, 5, 5, 5) sts bef the DS, turn.
Short Row 4 (WS): MDS, slipping BOR m, p to 2 (2, 3, 3, 3) (5, 5, 5, 5) sts bef the DS, turn.
Rep short rows 3 and 4, 0 (0, 1, 1, 1) (2, 2, 2, 2) more times.

Next Short Row (RS): MDS, k to 3 (3, 5, 5, 5) (7, 7, 7, 7) sts bef the DS, turn.
Next Short Row (WS): MDS, p to 3 (3, 5, 5, 5) (7, 7, 7, 7) sts bef the DS, turn.
Next Row (RS): MDS, k to BOR.
Next Rnd: K to end, working the DSs as one (like a k2tog). [144 (158, 168, 182, 198) (216, 230, 244, 260) sts]
K 0 (2, 2, 5, 5) (9, 13, 17, 20) rnd(s).
Adjustment Rnd: K11 (12, 13, 13, 10) (5, 10, 6, 4), *k2tog, k22 (17, 26, 20, 14) (10, 9, 9, 8)* to last 13 (13, 15, 15, 12) (7, 11, 7, 6) sts, k2tog, k11 (11, 13, 13, 10) (5, 9, 5, 4). [138 (150, 162, 174, 186) (198, 210, 222, 234) sts]

BEGIN YOKE PATT
Change to 16" / 40 cm circular needles or set of DPNs as necessary.

Beg working yoke patt from the Chart specified for your size, working the 6-st rep 23 (25, 27, 29, 31) (33, 35, 37, 39) times around, and working decs where indicated until all rnds of chart are complete. [92 (100, 81, 87, 93) (99, 105, 111, 117) sts]
Break C and D.

Sizes 0–3 mos and 3–6 mos only
Adjustment Rnd: With B, k2 (1, –, –, –) (–, –, –, –), *k2tog,
k1* to last 0 (2, –, –, –) (–, –, –, –) sts, k to end. [62 (68, –,
–, –) (–, –, –, –) sts]

Sizes 6–12 mos and 12–18 mos only
Adjustment Rnd: With B, k– (–, 4, 7 –, –, –, –), *k2tog,
k5* to last – (–, 0, 3, –) (–, –, –, –) sts, k to end. [– (–, 70,
76, –) (–, –, –, –) sts]

Sizes 2 yr, 4 yr, 6 yr, 8 yr and 10 yr only
Adjustment Rnd: With B, *k1, k2tog* – (–, –, –, 9) (10, 12,
14, 16) times, k – (–, –, –, 18) (18, 15, 12, 9), *k1, k2tog* –
(–, –, –, 10) (11, 13, 15, 17) times, k – (–, –, –, 18) (18, 15, 12,
9). [– (–, –, –, 74) (78, 80, 82, 84) sts]

Sizes 0–3 mos, 3–6 mos, 6–12 mos and 12–18 mos only
With US 5 / 3.75 mm 16" / 40 cm circular needles and B,
begin working back and forth as foll:
Row 1 (WS): Turn work so that WS is facing, *k1, p1* to
end, using Backwards Loop Method, CO 3 sts. [65 (71,
73, 79, –) (–, –, –, –) sts]
Row 2 (RS): K2, *p1, k1* to last 3 sts p1, k2.
Row 3 (WS): P2, *k1, p1* to last 3 sts, k1, p2.
Row 4 (make buttonhole): K2, yo, k2tog, *p1, k1* to last
3 sts, p1, k2.
Row 5: As row 3.
Row 6: As row 2.
BO loosely in rib patt.

Sizes 2 yr, 4 yr, 6 yr, 8 yr and 10 yr only
With US 5 / 3.75 mm set of DPNs or preferred needles
for small circumference knitting and B, work as foll:
Rnd 1: *K1, p1* to end.
Cont in est 1 x 1 rib for 5 more rnds.
BO loosely in 1 x 1 rib patt.

FINISHING

Use 3-Needle Bind-Off or Grafting to join underarm
sts. Weave in ends, closing any gaps that remain at the
underarms. Sizes 0–3 mos, 3–6 mos, 6–12 mos and
12–18 mos sew button to correspond to buttonhole on
neckband. Block to measurements.

YOKE CHART
Sizes 0–3 mos and 3–6 mos only

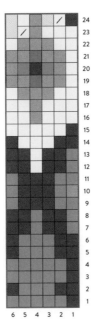

YOKE CHART
Sizes 6–12 mos, 12–18 mos, 2, 4, 6, 8 and 10 yrs only

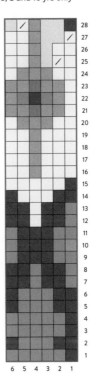

colour A

colour B

colour C

colour D

k2tog

pattern repeat

no stitch

ACKNOWLEDGEMENTS

FOR ME, KNITTING is a solitary activity. There are those long, still nights — tranquil nights, I would say — when the only sounds are the ones of my needles and my breathing. Everyone else in the household has gone to sleep and the time is truly mine to use as I wish: to doodle a design on my sketchpad or to play with colour combinations of yarns from my stash or to simply knit something with the anticipation of seeing how it turns out. If someone asked me why I design and knit things, I would probably say because the process not only gives me pleasure but also because it is one of those few moments in my life when I can find long, uninterrupted stretches of tranquility.

AT THE SAME time, I must admit that I love the communal aspects of designing, knitting and writing books. Indeed, the social part energises me in a myriad of different ways, and my community of friends and colleagues enable me to translate the ideas in my head into a knitted garment, then to a pattern and finally to a book. There have been many nights where my tranquility is interrupted by an idea — an idea that needs to be shared as soon as possible. If this moment arrives before 4 am, and it involves any type of stitchwork or felting, I usually call my good friend Midori Sakurai Miller as I know that she will be up (you can see some of Midori's stitchwork and felting in this book). And if it happens after 11 pm and involves all things knitting, I usually tap out a text message to my good friend Nikoleta Nutley and ask her to 'please, please' call me as soon as she gets up! If these two measures don't completely soothe me, I wait somewhat impatiently for my partner to get up — he is an early riser and usually starts his work by around 5 am. To be completely honest, I sometimes try to prompt his rising by making small noises that wake him from his slumbers, but are gentle enough not to put him in too bad a mood because he has been woken, so to speak.

THE PROCESS OF turning ideas into a knitting book involves more people and more discrete tasks than simply a phone call or text message. While almost all the knitted items contained in the book were first knit by me, Nikoleta helped me to finish a sleeve or a collar when I was rushed. I am grateful to Terri Maue, who did the technical editing and grading of the patterns, and to Sareena Granger who gave the patterns a final polish. Additionally, Teresa Allan, Linda Brett and Alina Velieva helped with the test knitting. Katie Harrison helped with a sock pattern and pullover pattern as well as with the test knitting. These interactions were both instrumental and social. They were instrumental in that they often improved the finished product. At the same time, these conversations energised me and reminded me that we are never alone when we have a passion that is shared. This is also true about the many people who have knit my previous patterns and provided words of encouragement and feedback: I am truly grateful for this.

THERE WAS A famous philosopher who once tried to articulate how he wrote such good books. In the knitting world, part of the answer to this question is having a great publisher who both believes in the book and takes a group of patterns and garments and turns them into something beautiful. I have been very lucky to have the opportunity to work with Jonna Hietala and Sini Kramer and the rest of the team at Laine Publishing. I have always admired the aesthetic of their magazines and books, so I was over the moon to have the opportunity to publish this book with them. Jonna shared my enthusiasm for the project and helped me — via multiple phone conversations and during her visits to Canada — to work through and refine the vision for the book. Sini was very organised and patient, helping to ensure that the book came to fruition. Anna Wallendahr and Jonna brought the patterns to life with their magical photos and finally, Tiina Vaarakallio used her graphic design skills to package everything together into a book that demonstrates the love and care that went into every step of the process. Seela Hietala contributed the handwritten texts and drawings: contributions that not only made me smile and laugh but also reminded me of the sheer delight of having children and grandchildren around! Finally, team Laine has provided just the right amount of hand-holding and gentle cajoling to get the book over the finish line!

GIVEN THAT THIS book is about knitting for children, it is not surprising that it is also a family affair. As I noted in the introduction, it was family — mamá Nela and mamá Elsa as well as tía Marta and tía Ana — that inspired and enabled my creative activities when I was a child. And my children, Oscar and Claudia, along with my partner, participated in this book, as they did with my previous knitting book. Oscar contributed his drawing skills and design know-how, while Claudia helped to write the introduction to the book as well as the introductions to the different patterns. They also inspired me to imagine what garments I would want to make for my grandchildren when that moment arrives. My partner is a different type of enabler. Simply put, he gave me the space to be myself — including waking him in the wee hours of the morning if necessary — and to not be overly encumbered with more mundane household tasks (smile).

IN CONCLUSION, I am sure that I have forgotten to acknowledge someone, because it takes a community to both raise a child and produce a knitting book. *Un abrazo* to all of you!

Claudia Q.

let's go!

This edition published in 2024 by Hardie Grant Books, an imprint of Hardie Grant Publishing
First published in 2023 by Laine Publishing Oy
Published by arrangement with Rights & Brands

Hardie Grant Books (Melbourne)
Wurundjeri Country
Building 1, 658 Church Street
Richmond, Victoria 3121

Hardie Grant Books (London)
5th & 6th Floors
52–54 Southwark Street
London SE1 1UN

hardiegrant.com/books

A catalogue record for this book is available from the National Library of Australia

Making Memories
ISBN 978 1 76145 039 6

10 9 8 7 6 5 4 3 2 1

Text & patterns: Claudia Quintanilla
Photography: Jonna Hietala & Anna Wallendahr
Illustrations: Seela Hietala
Graphic design: Tiina Vaarakallio
Stylist: Emilia Laitanen
Models: Amanda & Arvi, Anja & Ilana / BookUs
Clothes: Claudia Q, Kaiko Clothing, Louis Misha, Wheat, Wildkind Kids

Colour reproduction by Splitting Image Colour Studio
Printed in China by Leo Paper Products LTD.

The paper this book is printed on is from FSC®-certified forests and other sources. FSC® promotes environmentally responsible, socially beneficial and economically viable management of the world's forests.